AF442937

no straight line

Terrell Grier
No Straight Line

Copyright © 2025 by Terrell Grier
All rights reserved.
No part of this book may be reproduced in any form or by any electronic or mechanical
means, including information storage and retrieval systems, without written permission
from the author, except for the use of brief quotations in a book review.

ISBN 979-8-89691-514-0

no straight line

terrell grier

contents

Introduction   vii

1. The Beginning of a Legacy   1
2. The First Hustle   3
3. Building Connections   5
4. Grandma B's Influence   8
5. Meeting My Father   11
6. Sunday Dinner   14
7. Lessons from Big Daddy   17
8. Pops Teaches Respect   20
9. First Day in the New Hood   23
10. Exploring the Neighborhood   26
11. The Thrift Store Lesson   29
12. Big Mama's Values   32
13. Early Morning Discipline   35
14. Riding with Q   38
15. Fishing with Pops and TB   41
16. The Night of the Dice Game   45
17. A Walk Through Glenwood   47
18. The Risky Lick   50
19. Smoke's Lesson   53
20. Crossing the Line   56
21. A Moment of Clarity   59
22. Tornado on Hickory Street   62
23. The Price of Survival   65
24. Childhood Roots and Survival   66
25. Lessons from the Streets   68
26. Turning Point – Music as Salvation   69
27. The Fight for My Family   70
28. From Novara Street to Nottingham – The Rise of Casino
    Cuz'o   71
29. The Weight of Loyalty   77
30. Blood, Dice, and Survival   80
31. Lessons in Loyalty and Loss   83
32. The Funeral That Changed Everything   86
33. Survival Ain't Free   89
34. The Crossroads of Destiny   93

35. All In or Nothing   97
36. Building the Blueprint   101
37. From Vision to Reality   105
38. When Purpose Outgrew the Pain   109
39. The Fire Within   113
40. The Weight of the Mission   117
41. Bridges and Burdens   121
42. The Night Everything Almost Ended   125
43. The Weight of Silence   130
44. The Business of Survival   135
45. The Mirror and the Mask   139
46. The Burden of Forgiveness   143
47. When the World Stops Listening   148
48. The Legacy Blueprint   152
49. The Final Chapter – But Not the End   156
Epilogue   161

introduction

There are moments in life when the world stops—when everything you thought you knew, every plan you ever made, every version of the future you imagined, shatters into a million pieces. For me, those moments weren't rare. They were constant. They were gunshots echoing on street corners, the sound of glass breaking as I flew through a windshield, and the silence of an empty home where my children's laughter used to live.

But I'm still here. And if you're holding this book, so are you.

This isn't just a story—it's a lifeline. These words carry the weight of generations, the scars of survival, and the heartbeat of hope. I didn't write this book to entertain you. I wrote it because someone out there, maybe even you, is standing at a crossroads, wondering if it's worth it to keep going. And if my story can light a fire in your chest, if it can make you believe in yourself for one more day, then every risk I ever took was worth it.

You're about to step into my world—a world where dice games decided who walked away with a pocket full of cash and who went home empty. A world where funerals outnumbered birthdays and love had to be carved out of concrete and chaos. But it's also a world where dreams were born, where resilience became a second skin, and where the purest kind of love—love for family, love for freedom, love for the future—kept me breathing when I had every reason to quit.

This isn't a sanitized version of the truth. There's no sugarcoating here, no polishing away the grit and grime. You'll feel the weight of loss, the sharp edge of betrayal, and the flicker of hope that refuses to die. And through it all, I'll be here with you, guiding you through every chapter, every heartbreak, every victory.

I want you to read this book and see not just where I've been, but where *you* can go. Because if I can survive the streets, the scars, and the silence, then you can survive whatever you're facing, too.

So take a deep breath. Turn the page.

Because this isn't just my story—it's yours now, too.

Let's begin.

1

the beginning of a legacy

The humid Detroit night clung to the air like a second skin, carrying the smells of motor oil, barbecue, and dreams deferred. It was a time when the city pulsed with the rhythm of ambition, where hustlers and dreamers carved their paths amid the chaos. The Big Three automakers were on a decline, but the people of Detroit found ways to thrive despite the odds.

In the heart of this urban jungle, the gambling house on 7 Mile buzzed with the electric hum of voices and dice skidding across wooden tables. The room was packed, the air thick with cigar smoke and the scent of cheap cologne. Amid the clamor, the door swung open, and [Moms] walked in, her presence cutting through the noise like a knife through butter.

A young woman with fierce determination in her eyes, she had grown up around the game, understanding the rules of survival long before she understood her multiplication tables. The room fell silent for a moment as she entered, her confidence arresting the attention of even the most seasoned gamblers.

At the center of the room was Pops, a smooth-talking hustler whose every move oozed confidence. The dice in his hand rolled like extensions of his will, each throw a calculated risk that paid off more often than not. He was the kind of man who could walk into any room and make it his own—and tonight, this was his domain.

Their eyes locked, a charged moment that felt larger than the space it occupied. For a split second, the chaos of the room faded into the background, and all that existed was the undeniable pull between them. Pops motioned for Moms to place her bet with him, his voice low and smooth, "Bet with me, baby—you won't regret it."

There was something about the way he said it, the certainty in his tone, that made her trust him. She slid her money onto the table, her bet aligned with his, and the dice rolled. The room erupted in cheers as Pops hit his point, and Moms couldn't help but smile at the unexpected thrill.

By the end of the night, they weren't just strangers who'd crossed paths—they were two halves of the same hustle. Their bond was forged in the heat of the moment, a connection that promised more than just fleeting excitement. Little did they know that night would set the foundation for a legacy.

Moms and Pops began hustling together, their partnership a blend of calculated risks and unwavering ambition. Not long after, their union brought a son into the world—a boy born into the rhythm of the streets, destined to carry their combined fire and determination.

2

the first hustle

The streets of Detroit were more than pavement—they were a living, breathing entity that shaped everyone who walked them. For the narrator, those streets were both a playground and a battleground, a place where survival wasn't guaranteed but earned. It was here, amidst the clamor of car horns and the hum of streetlights, that he learned his first lesson in hustle.

It was a warm Saturday morning, the kind where the air carried the scent of freshly cut grass mingled with motor oil from nearby garages. At thirteen, the narrator wasn't thinking about school or chores—he was thinking about making money. He had watched older kids shooting dice in the alley behind the corner store, their voices rising in laughter and anger as the dice rolled across the cracked pavement.

He had seen how they walked away with pockets full of cash, and something about the way they moved, with a confidence that came from owning their fate, pulled him in.

The First Dice Game

"I gotta make something happen today," he thought as he approached the alley, clutching the only $5 bill he had to his name. Smoke, his older friend and mentor of sorts, was already there, leaning against the wall with a cigarette dangling from his lips.

"You ready for this, little bro?" Smoke asked, a sly grin on his face.

"Yeah, I'm ready," the narrator replied, trying to hide the tremor in his voice.

Smoke slapped a $10 bill into the narrator's hand. "Here's the deal: you roll for me first. Watch how I play this."

The narrator nodded, his heart pounding as he stepped into the circle of older boys. The dice felt foreign in his hands, heavier than he expected, but the weight felt good. He rolled, and the dice tumbled across the ground. A hush fell over the group as they came to a stop.

"Seven! That's my boy!" Smoke shouted, clapping him on the back.

The narrator couldn't help but smile, the thrill of the win washing over him. The other boys grumbled, tossing money onto the ground for the next roll. With each throw, the narrator grew bolder, his confidence swelling as he watched the pile of cash grow.

A Taste of Power

By the end of the game, they had turned that $10 into $60—a small fortune for a kid his age. Smoke handed him $20 as they walked away from the alley. "You did good, little bro. Real good. But remember, the streets don't love nobody. You gotta keep your head on straight."

The narrator pocketed the money, the weight of the cash making him feel taller, stronger. It wasn't just about the money—it was about what it represented: independence, power, and a taste of something he'd been chasing without knowing it. He realized then that the hustle wasn't just a game—it was a way of life.

The Cost of the Hustle

That night, as he lay in bed, the narrator replayed the dice game in his mind. The rush of winning, the camaraderie of the circle, the thrill of taking a risk—it all felt intoxicating. But beneath the excitement, a small voice in the back of his mind whispered a warning: "What happens when you lose?"

He pushed the thought away, choosing instead to focus on the possibilities. For now, he was on top, and that was enough.

3

building connections

$\mathscr{I}$n the streets of Detroit, connections weren't just helpful—they were essential. The narrator learned early on that who you knew often determined how far you could go. Relationships were currency, traded as skillfully as dice rolls and hustles. But trust was a rare commodity, forged only through shared struggles and tested loyalty.

The Basketball Court Brotherhood

The local basketball court was more than a place for games; it was a meeting ground, a proving ground, and a sanctuary. The narrator spent countless afternoons there, perfecting his shot and watching the unspoken hierarchies unfold. There were the stars—players whose moves earned respect—and then there were the watchers, those who knew the real game was off the court.

"Yo, Rell!" shouted Smoke, waving him over from the sidelines. "You see P over there? That's the kind of guy you want to know."

P was a neighborhood legend, a tall, wiry kid with a mean jump shot and a reputation for helping his people. The narrator approached cautiously, unsure of how to break into the inner circle.

"You got game, little man?" P asked, tossing the ball his way.

The narrator nodded, swallowing his nerves. "Yeah, I can play."

By the end of the game, the narrator had earned more than a win—he'd earned P's respect. It was the beginning of a bond that would shape his understanding of loyalty and hierarchy.

The Dice Game Diplomacy

Away from the courts, the alley dice games were another arena for building connections. These games weren't just about money; they were about reputation. The narrator learned to watch carefully, picking up on who was bluffing, who was backing their bets, and who was silently calling the shots.

One day, while rolling dice with Smoke and a group of older players, a dispute broke out. Tensions flared as one player accused another of cheating. Voices rose, and the atmosphere turned electric with potential violence.

"Chill out," the narrator said, stepping between the two men. "Ain't no need for all that. Let's just roll it out."

His calm demeanor and quick thinking diffused the situation, earning nods of approval from the group. It was a small moment, but one that cemented his reputation as someone who could handle pressure—a valuable trait in a world where trust was always in short supply.

Navigating the Social Web

The narrator's world was a delicate balance of alliances and rivalries. He learned to navigate it with precision, understanding when to align himself with certain people and when to step back. Each connection he made, whether through basketball games, dice rolls, or quiet conversations on the corner, was another thread in the web that held his life together.

But with every connection came a cost. The deeper he got into this world, the more he realized that loyalty was a double-edged sword. To some, loyalty meant support and protection. To others, it meant a debt that could never be repaid.

The Mentor Figures

Smoke and P were two of the most significant figures in the narrator's life during this time. Smoke taught him the rules of the hustle, the importance of staying sharp and keeping your eyes open. P, on the other hand, showed him the value of community, of looking out for your people even when the odds were stacked against you.

"Always remember, Rell," P said one night as they sat on the stoop, "you're only as good as the people you keep around you. Choose wisely."

Those words stayed with the narrator, a guiding principle in a world where trust could mean the difference between success and survival.

The First Betrayal

Connections weren't always reliable. One day, a friend the narrator had trusted betrayed him during a dice game, pocketing money that wasn't his. The sting of betrayal cut deep, but it was a lesson the narrator would never forget: not all friendships were built to last.

"That's on me," he told Smoke later. "Should've seen it coming."

"Nah," Smoke replied, lighting a cigarette. "That's on him. But now you know—always watch your back."

4
grandma b's influence

The smell of biscuits baking in the oven and the faint hum of an old Motown record filled Grandma B's kitchen. This wasn't just a place to cook—it was a sanctuary, a classroom, and the heart of the family. For the narrator, every visit to Grandma B's house was an experience in love, resilience, and quiet wisdom. She didn't teach lessons with lectures; she taught them with actions, with the way she carried herself and cared for others.

The Kitchen as a Sanctuary

The narrator always felt safe in Grandma B's kitchen, a stark contrast to the chaos of the streets outside. The counters were cluttered but clean, with jars of flour and sugar lined up next to a collection of well-worn cookbooks. A pot of greens simmered on the stove, the smell mingling with the aroma of freshly brewed coffee.

"Baby, wash your hands before you touch anything," Grandma B said, her voice firm but kind.

"Yes, ma'am," the narrator replied, obeying without hesitation. In her presence, respect wasn't demanded—it was earned. She had a way of making you want to be better, to rise to her expectations without feeling forced.

The First Lesson: Every Dollar Counts

One summer afternoon, Grandma B took the narrator to the thrift store. He had been reluctant to go at first, embarrassed by the idea of shopping second-hand. But Grandma B had a way of turning everything into an adventure.

"See this?" she said, holding up a pair of jeans that looked brand new. "These cost $5 here. In the mall, they'd be $50. Now, tell me what makes more sense."

The narrator nodded, slowly beginning to understand. It wasn't about being flashy or keeping up appearances—it was about making smart choices. By the time they left the store, his perspective had shifted. He realized that value wasn't always tied to price.

The Garden of Wisdom

Grandma B had a small garden in her backyard, a patch of earth where she grew tomatoes, collard greens, and herbs. She often brought the narrator out there to help her tend to the plants.

"See these weeds?" she asked one day, pointing to a patch of grass encroaching on her tomatoes. "If you don't pull them out, they'll choke the life out of the good stuff."

The narrator nodded, pulling at the weeds with his hands. Later, he realized that Grandma B wasn't just talking about gardening—she was talking about life. The weeds were the distractions, the negativity, and the bad influences that could derail your path if you let them.

The Gift of Resilience

Grandma B had seen her share of hardships, from raising children during tough economic times to losing loved ones to the streets. But she never let the weight of the world crush her spirit. She carried herself with a quiet strength that inspired everyone around her.

"You don't get stronger by avoiding hard times," she told the narrator one evening. "You get stronger by facing them, by working through them."

Those words stayed with him, a mantra he would repeat to himself during his own struggles. In many ways, Grandma B was the anchor that kept him grounded, the example he looked to when the world felt too overwhelming.

The Sunday Dinner Ritual

Every Sunday, the family gathered at Grandma B's house for

dinner. The table was always full—fried chicken, macaroni and cheese, cornbread, and greens—and so was the house, with laughter and conversation filling every corner.

But Sunday dinners weren't just about food. They were about connection, about taking a moment to appreciate each other despite the chaos of life. Grandma B presided over these meals like a queen, her presence commanding respect and gratitude.

"Eat up, baby," she would say, handing the narrator a plate piled high with food. "You can't face the world on an empty stomach."

A Quiet Goodbye

One day, as the narrator grew older and life pulled him further into the streets, he realized he hadn't visited Grandma B in weeks. When he finally made it back to her house, she was sitting on the porch, her hands folded in her lap.

"Took you long enough," she said, her tone teasing but her eyes full of warmth.

At that moment, the narrator understood the depth of her love. No matter how far he strayed, Grandma B would always be there, her door open, her heart ready to welcome him back.

5
meeting my father

The narrator had spent years wondering about his father. His mother's stories were fragments, glimpses into a man who felt more like a shadow than a person. He knew the basics: his father had been absent for most of his life, caught up in the chaos of a system that seemed to take more than it gave. But curiosity lived in the spaces between the facts, and it wasn't until that fateful day that he would come face-to-face with the man who had been missing from his life for so long.

The Moment of Truth

The day was overcast, the sky heavy with gray clouds that seemed to mirror the narrator's emotions—equal parts anticipation and anxiety. He sat in the passenger seat of Grandma B's car, his hands fidgeting with the fraying threads on his jeans.

"Baby," Grandma B said, her voice breaking the silence, "you ready to meet your daddy?"

The narrator hesitated, his throat tightening. He nodded, not trusting his voice to speak.

As they pulled up to the large two-family flat, his heart raced. The house was alive with movement, children playing on the porch, the smell of soul food wafting from the kitchen window. The front door creaked open and out stepped his father—a tall, dark-skinned man with a strong jawline and eyes that carried stories untold.

The First Encounter

The narrator froze, his breath catching in his chest. His father's gaze locked onto him, a mixture of recognition and disbelief crossing his face. For a moment, the world stood still. Then, his father's expression softened, and he extended a hand.

"You must be my boy," he said, his voice deep and steady. "No need for a DNA test. You're the spitting image of me."

The narrator shook his father's hand, the warmth and firmness of his grip grounding him in the moment. It wasn't the embrace he'd dreamed of, but it was something—a start.

Inside the House

The house was bustling with activity, the air thick with the scent of collard greens and fried chicken. The narrator was ushered inside, where faces he didn't recognize greeted him like long-lost family. His grandmother, Big Mama, pulled him into a hug that felt like home.

"Welcome, baby," she said, her voice full of emotion. "You've been a part of this family from the start, whether you knew it or not."

The narrator was led to the dining table, where plates of food were already being served. His father sat beside him, his presence both comforting and intimidating. They didn't speak much at first, but the unspoken connection between them was palpable.

The First Conversation

After dinner, the two of them stepped outside to sit on the porch. The narrator stared at the ground, unsure of how to start. His father broke the silence.

"I know I wasn't there for you," he said, his voice heavy with regret. "Life didn't go the way I planned. But I want to make it right, starting now."

The narrator looked up, meeting his father's eyes. "Why weren't you there?" he asked, his voice trembling.

His father sighed, the weight of the question settling over him. "I made mistakes. Got caught up in things I shouldn't have. But that's no excuse. You deserved better."

For the first time, the narrator saw his father not as a figure of absence, but as a man—flawed, human, and trying.

Building the Bridge

Over the next few hours, they talked about everything and nothing. His father shared stories of his youth, tales of mischief and hard lessons learned. The narrator listened, hanging on every word, piecing together the puzzle of the man before him.

"I'm not perfect," his father admitted. "But I'm here now. And I'm not going anywhere."

The Promise

As the day came to an end, the narrator felt a strange mix of emotions—anger for the years lost, hope for the future, and a cautious optimism that maybe, just maybe, things could be different.

His father placed a hand on his shoulder. "We've got a lot to catch up on, son. But we'll take it one day at a time."

The narrator nodded, a small smile forming on his lips. For the first time, he felt like he wasn't alone.

6
sunday dinner

The smell of collard greens, baked macaroni and cheese, and cornbread wafted through Big Mama's house. Sunday dinner was more than just a meal—it was a ritual, a celebration of family and survival. Every dish carried a story, every bite a reminder of the strength it took to get through the week. For the narrator, these dinners were a temporary reprieve from the chaos of life outside.

The Arrival

The narrator stepped onto the porch, his senses immediately overwhelmed by the sounds and smells of home. Big Mama's laughter boomed from the kitchen, a sound as warm as the food she was cooking. Kids ran around the living room, dodging legs and shrieking with joy, while the older men played cards at the dining table.

"Rell, you better get in here before all this food's gone!" Big Mama called from the kitchen.

The narrator walked inside, his stomach growling as the aroma of fried chicken hit him. He greeted his aunts, uncles, and cousins, feeling a sense of belonging that was rare in his world.

The Feast

The table was a masterpiece. Platters of golden fried chicken, buttery cornbread, sweet yams, and Big Mama's signature greens covered every inch. The narrator's mouth watered as he took his seat, the chatter of family creating a symphony around him.

Big Mama stood at the head of the table, her presence commanding respect. "Before we eat, let's say grace," she said, bowing her head.

The room fell silent as Uncle Junior led the prayer, his voice steady and deep. When the "Amen" came, the sound of plates clinking and voices laughing filled the room.

"Pass them yams this way," someone shouted.

"Don't be greedy, now!" Big Mama teased, her laughter contagious.

Conversations Over Food

Sunday dinner wasn't just about eating—it was about connection. As plates were filled and refilled, stories began to flow. The uncles shared tales of their youth, exaggerated for effect, while the cousins cracked jokes and debated who had the best dance moves.

"Rell," Uncle Junior said, pointing a fork at him. "You still running around with that boy Smoke? You know he ain't nothing but trouble."

The narrator hesitated, his fork hovering over his plate. "Smoke's alright, Uncle Junior. He just does what he has to."

Big Mama shot him a look, her eyes piercing. "Just remember, baby, you are who you hang with. Don't let nobody drag you down."

Her words stayed with him, a quiet reminder that his choices mattered more than he realized.

A Moment of Reflection

As the meal wound down, the older folks moved to the living room, their laughter echoing as they settled into comfortable chairs. The narrator stayed behind, helping Big Mama clear the table.

"Thank you for coming, baby," she said, placing a hand on his shoulder. "It's important to stay close to your people. Family is all we got in this world."

He nodded, her words settling into the cracks of his heart.

The Aftermath

By the time the narrator left, the sun had set, casting a warm glow over the neighborhood. The night was quiet, the kind of peace that felt fleeting in a city that never truly slept.

As he walked home, he replayed the day in his mind—the food, the laughter, the love that filled Big Mama's house. It wasn't perfect, but it was enough to remind him of what he was fighting for.

16

7

lessons from big daddy

*B*ig Daddy wasn't a man of many words, but when he spoke, his voice carried the weight of a thousand lessons. He was a towering figure in the narrator's life—firm, unyielding, and quietly loving. Big Daddy believed in hard work, discipline, and respect, values he passed down through actions rather than speeches. For the narrator, spending time with Big Daddy was like attending an unspoken school of life, where every task was a lesson and every word carried a deeper meaning.

The Morning Wake-Up Call

The sun had barely risen when the narrator was startled awake by the deep rumble of Big Daddy's voice echoing through the house.

"Up and at it, boy! We got work to do!"

The narrator groaned, rubbing the sleep from his eyes. It was a Saturday—his one day to sleep in—but Big Daddy had other plans.

When he stumbled into the kitchen, the smell of coffee and fresh biscuits greeted him. Big Daddy was already dressed, his overalls stained with years of labor, his hands rough from decades of hard work.

"Eat quick," Big Daddy said, nodding toward the plate on the table. "We got a long day ahead."

The Yard Work Lesson

Their first task of the day was clearing debris from the backyard—a seemingly simple chore that became a masterclass in patience and perseverance.

"Pick it all up," Big Daddy instructed, pointing to the scattered branches and leaves. "Don't leave nothing behind."

The narrator worked diligently, sweat dripping from his brow as the morning sun climbed higher. When he thought he was done, Big Daddy walked over and silently pointed to a small pile of twigs he'd missed.

"Details matter," he said, his voice calm but firm. "If you can't do the small things right, you'll never handle the big things."

The lesson wasn't lost on the narrator. It wasn't just about cleaning the yard—it was about taking pride in your work, no matter how menial the task seemed.

The Refrigerator Challenge

Later that day, Big Daddy decided it was time to move an old refrigerator from the basement to the upstairs porch. The narrator looked at the narrow staircase and doubted it was even possible.

"We can't do this," he said, shaking his head.

Big Daddy raised an eyebrow. "Can't ain't in my vocabulary, boy. Let's get to it."

The process was grueling. Every step was a struggle, the weight of the refrigerator pressing down on their shoulders. But Big Daddy didn't complain—he simply kept pushing, his determination unwavering.

By the time they finished, the narrator's arms ached, but a sense of accomplishment swelled in his chest.

"See?" Big Daddy said, clapping him on the back. "You're stronger than you think. Don't forget that."

The Quiet Moments

As the day wound down, they sat on the porch, sipping lemonade and watching the sun dip below the horizon. The narrator was too tired to speak, but Big Daddy didn't seem to mind the silence.

"Life ain't easy," Big Daddy said after a long pause. "But you don't get stronger by avoiding the hard stuff. You get stronger by facing it head-on."

The narrator nodded, the simplicity of the statement sinking in.

Big Daddy's Legacy

Big Daddy had come to Detroit from the South in the 1960s, bringing with him a work ethic forged in the fields and a determination to build a better life for his family. He worked multiple jobs, saved every penny, and bought the house they now lived in—a testament to his resilience and sacrifice.

"Everything I do, I do for family," he told the narrator. "One day, you'll understand what that means."

A Lesson in Respect

The narrator learned that respect wasn't just given—it was earned. Big Daddy treated everyone with fairness, but he didn't tolerate laziness or disrespect.

One day, when a neighbor spoke harshly to Big Mama, Big Daddy calmly stepped in.

"Apologize," he said, his voice low but firm. The neighbor hesitated, but the quiet intensity in Big Daddy's gaze left no room for argument.

The narrator watched, understanding for the first time that true strength didn't require shouting or threats—it came from self-control and confidence.

8
pops teaches respect

Pops was a man who lived by a code. Respect wasn't a word to him—it was a way of life. In a world where trust was fragile and power often determined by who spoke the loudest, Pops stood out for his calm strength and unwavering principles. His lessons weren't just about how to survive the streets—they were about how to navigate life with dignity and a sense of purpose.

For the narrator, Pops' teachings would become a cornerstone of his journey, shaping how he moved through the world and how he saw himself.

The Dice Game That Changed Everything

It was a humid summer evening, and Pops had invited the narrator to join him at a local dice game. The crowd gathered on the porch was a mix of seasoned gamblers, hustlers, and young men eager to make a name for themselves. The atmosphere buzzed with energy, the clatter of dice hitting wood punctuated by shouts and laughter.

"Watch and learn," Pops said, handing the narrator a folding chair.

Pops approached the game with the quiet confidence of a man who had nothing to prove. He didn't rush his rolls or try to outtalk the other players. Instead, he let his skill and composure do the talking.

"You see that?" Pops asked after hitting his point with a flawless roll. "They respect the man who knows his craft and keeps his cool. That's how you win—not just the game, but in life."

The Confrontation

As the night wore on, tension brewed between Pops and another player—a brash young man who didn't take losing well. When Pops collected his winnings after a particularly lucky roll, the man stood up, his voice rising above the crowd.

"You think you're slick, old man?" he said, his tone challenging. "Bet you wouldn't be so cocky without your little lucky streak."

The narrator froze, expecting Pops to react with anger. Instead, Pops remained seated, his expression calm.

"Son," Pops said, his voice low but firm, "luck ain't got nothing to do with it. If you think I'm wrong, let the dice decide."

The man hesitated, his bravado faltering under Pops' steady gaze. Without another word, he sat back down, the respect in his silence louder than any apology.

"See that?" Pops said to the narrator later. "Respect ain't about being the loudest or the strongest. It's about knowing who you are and not letting anyone shake that."

The Lesson in Generosity

After the game, Pops handed the narrator $300 from his winnings.

"Take this," he said. "But remember—money don't make the man. How you use it does."

The narrator spent days thinking about those words. Pops didn't flaunt his success or use it to belittle others. Instead, he shared what he had, lifting up those around him. It was a quiet lesson in generosity, one that left a lasting impression.

Earning Respect

Pops' teachings extended beyond the dice game. One afternoon, the narrator accompanied him to a neighborhood barbecue. As they walked through the crowd, people greeted Pops with nods and handshakes, their respect for him evident in every interaction.

"Why do they all look up to you?" the narrator asked.

"Because I give them a reason to," Pops replied. "I treat people right, even when they don't deserve it. And I don't take nothing I didn't earn."

The Night It All Clicked

Weeks later, the narrator found himself in a heated argument with a friend over a dice game. Voices were raised, tempers flared, and for a moment, the narrator considered throwing a punch. But then he remembered Pops' words: "Respect ain't about being the loudest or the strongest."

Taking a deep breath, he stepped back. "You win," he said, walking away from the game.

That night, Pops clapped him on the shoulder. "You learned the most important lesson of all, son," he said. "Sometimes, the best way to win is to walk away."

9

first day in the new hood

The first day in a new neighborhood is like stepping onto an unfamiliar battlefield. Every glance, every interaction, feels like a test, a silent challenge to prove you belong. For the narrator, moving into his father's neighborhood wasn't just about adjusting to a new house—it was about learning a new set of unspoken rules. The streets carried their own rhythm, and fitting in meant adapting quickly.

The Walk Around the Block

The morning after moving in, the narrator decided to explore. The sun was just rising, casting long shadows across the cracked sidewalks. Pops was already up, sitting on the porch with a coffee in hand.

"Where you headed, son?" Pops asked, his eyes following the narrator as he laced up his sneakers.

"Just walking around," the narrator replied, trying to sound casual.

"Alright," Pops said, nodding. "Keep your head on straight. And remember, this ain't just a neighborhood—it's a community. Respect it, and it'll respect you back."

With those words in mind, the narrator set off, his steps tentative as he took in his surroundings. The block was alive with activity. Kids played basketball on a milk crate hoop, their shouts echoing down the street. A group of older men leaned against a car, their conversation punctuated by bursts of laughter.

Meeting TB and the Crew

As he turned the corner, the narrator spotted his little brother TB in a crowd of kids near Big Mama's house. TB waved him over, his face lighting up with excitement.

"Yo, everybody! This my big brother!" TB announced, puffing out his chest with pride.

The group turned to look at the narrator, their expressions a mix of curiosity and skepticism. One boy, a lanky teen with a basketball under his arm, stepped forward.

"Can you hoop?" he asked, his tone challenging.

The narrator nodded. "Yeah, I can play."

The game that followed wasn't just about basketball—it was an initiation. Every shot, every pass, was a chance to prove himself. By the end of the game, he had earned their respect, his skill on the court speaking louder than words.

The First Test

Later that afternoon, the narrator and TB were sitting on the porch when a commotion erupted down the block. A group of teens was arguing over a dice game, their voices rising with each passing second.

"Yo, TB, what's going on over there?" the narrator asked.

"That's P and his crew," TB replied. "They run this block. If you're cool with them, you're good."

The narrator watched as P, the undisputed leader, diffused the situation with a few calm words and a steady gaze. There was something about the way P carried himself—a mix of confidence and authority—that reminded the narrator of Pops.

"Think he'll give me a shot?" the narrator asked.

TB shrugged. "You gotta earn it."

The Encounter with P

That evening, the narrator approached P during a dice game. The older boy looked him up and down, his expression unreadable.

"You Rell, right? Pops' kid?" P asked.

"Yeah," the narrator replied, trying to keep his voice steady.

P nodded, a hint of a smile tugging at his lips. "Your pops is good people. You stick around him, and you'll be alright. But don't think that gets you a free pass. Around here, respect is earned."

The narrator nodded, understanding the unspoken challenge in P's words. This was a test, and he was determined to pass.

The Lesson in Loyalty

Over the next few days, the narrator spent more time with P and his crew, learning the rhythms of the block. He quickly realized that loyalty was the foundation of their world. Everyone had each other's back, whether it was sharing food, splitting winnings, or standing up in a fight.

One afternoon, when a stranger wandered onto their block and started causing trouble, the crew rallied together, forcing the intruder to leave. The narrator watched in awe as P took charge, his calm authority diffusing the tension before it could escalate.

"You see that?" P said afterward, turning to the narrator. "This ain't about being tough. It's about being smart. If you can keep your head while everyone else is losing theirs, you'll always come out on top."

10
exploring the neighborhood

The neighborhood was alive in ways the narrator had never fully appreciated before. It wasn't just a collection of streets and houses—it was a world within itself, with its own rhythm, rules, and stories. Every corner held a new discovery, every block a different challenge. For the narrator, exploring the neighborhood wasn't just about finding his place—it was about understanding the environment that would shape him in ways he couldn't yet imagine.

The Basketball Court: A Gathering Place

One of the first places the narrator visited was the basketball court, where kids of all ages gathered daily. The court wasn't just a place to play—it was a hub of activity, a meeting ground for the neighborhood's younger generation.

"Yo, Rell, you hooping today?" TB asked, dribbling a weathered basketball.

The narrator nodded, joining a pickup game with a mix of kids he knew and some he didn't. The competition was fierce, but it was never just about winning. The court was where alliances were formed, rivalries were sparked, and respect was earned.

"You got a nice jump shot," one of the older boys said after the game, slapping the narrator on the back. "You might just fit in around here."

The Candy House

On another day, the narrator found himself drawn to Aunt Ruby's candy house, a neighborhood staple. Aunt Ruby's porch was always crowded with kids clutching coins, eager to trade them for bags of chips, candy, and juice.

"What you need, baby?" Aunt Ruby asked as the narrator stepped up to the window.

"Two juices and a bag of hot chips," he said, sliding his money across the counter.

Aunt Ruby handed him his snacks with a warm smile. "You're Pops' boy, ain't you? You tell him I said hi."

The candy house wasn't just about snacks—it was a place where the narrator began to feel the interconnectedness of the neighborhood, where everyone seemed to know everyone else.

The Bando: A Hidden World

Exploration also took the narrator to the abandoned houses, or "bandos," that dotted the neighborhood. These were more than just empty structures—they were places of adventure, danger, and intrigue.

One afternoon, P suggested a game of manhunt at one of the bandos. The narrator hesitated at first, but his curiosity won out. The group crept through the dark, creaking halls, their laughter echoing as they darted in and out of hiding spots.

"Don't get caught slipping," P warned with a grin, tagging the narrator as "out."

The bando was both thrilling and sobering—a stark reminder of the neighborhood's challenges, but also a place where the kids created their own moments of joy.

The Street Corners

The narrator quickly learned that every block had its own personality. Some corners were dominated by older guys playing cards or dice, their voices rising in playful banter. Others were quieter, marked by the hum of passing cars and the occasional bark of a dog.

One day, as the narrator walked down the block, he crossed paths with Pole Cat, a neighborhood legend known for climbing utility poles without safety gear to restore people's electricity.

"You need anything, young blood?" Pole Cat asked, wiping sweat from his brow.

"Nah, I'm good," the narrator replied, smiling.

"Good," Pole Cat said, nodding. "Keep it that way."

Interactions like these helped the narrator piece together the neighborhood's unwritten rules and the roles people played within it.

The First Threat

Not all of the neighborhood's lessons were positive. One evening, while walking home, the narrator encountered a group of boys dressed in red—clear members of a rival crew.

"What you doing around here, blue boy?" one of them asked, stepping forward.

The narrator's heart raced, but he stood his ground. Before the situation could escalate, TB and P appeared, their presence diffusing the tension.

"You messing with my brother?" TB asked, his voice calm but firm.

The group backed off, muttering under their breath as they walked away. The incident left the narrator shaken but grateful for the bond he was building with his new community.

11
the thrift store lesson

The thrift store wasn't just a place to shop—it was a classroom where Grandma B taught the narrator one of life's most valuable lessons: how to find worth in things others overlooked. For a kid growing up in a world where image often trumped substance, the thrift store was an unlikely but profound teacher.

The Journey to the Store

It was a warm Saturday afternoon when Grandma B announced they were going shopping. The narrator, expecting a trip to the mall, reluctantly agreed. Instead, they pulled into the parking lot of a thrift store, the faded sign above the entrance barely clinging to its letters.

"Why are we here?" the narrator asked, his disappointment evident.

Grandma B chuckled, patting his hand. "Because, baby, this is where you learn the difference between spending money and making it stretch."

The Hunt Begins

Inside, the store smelled faintly of mothballs and old fabric. Rows of clothing racks stretched across the space, each bursting with items of every size and color. To the narrator, it felt overwhelming and disorganized, but Grandma B moved with purpose.

"Look here," she said, holding up a shirt. "Brand new. Still got the tags on it, and it's only three dollars."

She handed it to the narrator, who inspected it with a mix of curiosity and skepticism. "Why's it so cheap?"

"Because somebody didn't want it anymore," Grandma B replied. "But that don't mean it ain't worth something."

The First Find

As they combed through the racks, the narrator stumbled upon a jacket that caught his eye—a black bomber with minimal wear. He hesitated, unsure if it was "cool enough."

"Try it on," Grandma B encouraged.

He slipped it on, glancing at himself in the mirror. It fit perfectly, and for the first time, he began to see the thrift store in a new light.

"This one's five bucks," he said, smiling.

Grandma B nodded. "Now you're getting it."

Life Lessons Between the Racks

As they continued shopping, Grandma B shared stories from her past. She spoke of growing up with little but always making the most of what she had.

"When I was your age, baby, we didn't have malls," she said. "We had hand-me-downs and homemade clothes. But we made it work. And you can, too."

The narrator listened intently, realizing that this trip wasn't just about clothes—it was about understanding the value of resourcefulness and gratitude.

At the Register

By the time they reached the register, their cart was full of treasures: shirts, pants, a pair of shoes, and even a hat. The total came to less than $20, a fraction of what they would have spent at the mall.

"See?" Grandma B said, handing over the cash. "You don't need to spend a lot to look good. You just need to know where to look."

The Ride Home

On the ride back, the narrator stared out the window, his mind racing with newfound appreciation. He realized that the thrift store wasn't just a place to save money—it was a place where value was hidden in plain sight, waiting to be discovered.

"Thank you, Grandma," he said softly.

She smiled, reaching over to pat his knee. "You're welcome, baby. Just remember—what matters ain't how much something costs. It's what you do with it."

12
big mama's values

ig Mama's home wasn't just a house—it was a foundation built on love, discipline, and unshakable principles. Everything about her, from the way she spoke to the meals she prepared, radiated a deep sense of purpose. For the narrator, time spent with Big Mama was a chance to learn about the unspoken values that guided the family and, by extension, his own life.

The Warmth of Home

Walking into Big Mama's house was like stepping into a sanctuary. The aroma of fresh-baked biscuits and slow-cooked greens greeted the narrator as he stepped through the door. On one particular day, Big Mama sat at the kitchen table, rolling dough with a precision that seemed effortless.

"You hungry, baby?" she asked, her tone soft but commanding.

The narrator nodded. "Always, Big Mama."

"Well, wash up first," she said, gesturing toward the sink. "Ain't no sense eating with dirty hands."

This wasn't just a reminder to wash—it was an introduction to one of Big Mama's core beliefs: cleanliness and preparation were non-negotiable, not just for meals but for life.

The Garden of Life

Behind Big Mama's house was her pride and joy—a garden bursting with collard greens, tomatoes, peppers, and herbs. She spent hours there, tending to each plant with care. One day, she handed the narrator a small spade.

"Help me weed this patch," she said, pointing to a corner where grass had begun to take over.

As they worked, she explained the significance of the task. "You see these weeds? They'll choke out the good plants if we let them. Same goes for life, baby. You gotta pull out the bad before it takes over."

The narrator nodded, the metaphor sinking in deeper with every handful of weeds he removed.

The Art of Gratitude

Mealtime at Big Mama's wasn't just about eating—it was about gratitude. Before every meal, she insisted on saying grace, her hands clasped tightly as she thanked God for their blessings.

"Ain't no shame in starting small," she said one evening as they ate. "What matters is being thankful for what you have and working for what you want."

The narrator watched as Big Mama dished out second helpings to everyone, her smile never fading. She made sure no one left the table hungry, embodying her belief in generosity and care.

Tough Love

Big Mama's kindness was matched by her firmness. She didn't tolerate laziness or disrespect, and she made sure the narrator understood that from a young age.

One afternoon, he came home with mud on his shoes, tracking it across her freshly mopped floor.

"Boy, you better get back outside and clean that mess up!" she snapped, her voice sharper than he'd ever heard it.

Embarrassed but obedient, he did as she said. Later, she pulled him aside.

"I ain't mad at you, baby," she said. "But if I let you get away with that, you'll think it's okay to leave a mess for someone else to clean up. And that's not how we do things in this house."

The Sewing Lesson

One evening, the narrator found Big Mama at her sewing machine, mending a torn shirt. She motioned for him to sit beside her.

"Life's like this shirt," she said, holding up the fabric. "It ain't always gonna stay perfect. But if you take the time to fix it, it'll last a lot longer."

As she stitched, she explained how every thread represented an opportunity to make something stronger, to repair what was broken instead of throwing it away.

The Unseen Burdens

What the narrator didn't fully understand at the time was the weight Big Mama carried. She had raised multiple generations, worked tirelessly to keep the family afloat, and endured hardships that she rarely spoke of.

One night, as he was leaving, he noticed her sitting on the porch, staring at the stars.

"You okay, Big Mama?" he asked.

She smiled faintly, her gaze never leaving the sky. "I'm always okay, baby. Don't you worry about me?"

But in her silence, he saw the strength it took to carry so much without complaint.

13
early morning discipline

For Big Daddy, mornings weren't a time for rest—they were a time for action. The sun didn't dictate his schedule; his sense of duty did. He believed in starting the day with purpose, and for the narrator, those early mornings were a mix of exhaustion, irritation, and invaluable life lessons.

Big Daddy's booming voice wasn't just a wake-up call—it was a command to rise and meet the day head-on, no matter how tired you were or how much you wanted to stay in bed.

The Wake-Up Call

"Get up, boy! Daylight's burning!"

The narrator jolted awake, his dreams dissolving into the reality of Big Daddy's voice echoing through the house. It was barely 6 a.m., and the sun hadn't fully risen. He groaned, throwing the covers over his head, but Big Daddy wasn't having it.

"I said get up!" Big Daddy called again, his footsteps heavy as he approached the bedroom door.

The narrator knew better than to argue. He rolled out of bed, rubbing the sleep from his eyes as he stumbled into the kitchen. Big Daddy was already there, his overalls on, his hands wrapped around a steaming cup of coffee.

"Wash your face, eat something, and let's get to it," he said, his tone leaving no room for negotiation.

Yard Work with a Lesson

Their first task was raking leaves in the yard. It seemed simple enough, but Big Daddy turned it into an exercise in precision.

"Don't just pile them up any kind of way," he said, demonstrating how to rake the leaves into neat rows. "Do it right the first time, or you'll have to do it all over again."

The narrator worked in silence, sweat dripping down his face as the morning sun grew hotter. When he thought he was finished, Big Daddy walked over and inspected his work, pointing out a few stray leaves he'd missed.

"See this?" Big Daddy said, picking up a leaf. "This might seem small, but small things add up. You leave this here, and next thing you know, the whole yard's a mess again."

The narrator sighed but went back to finish the job. It wasn't just about the leaves—it was about paying attention to details and taking pride in your work.

The Refrigerator Challenge

After the yard work, Big Daddy decided it was time to move an old refrigerator from the basement to the porch. The narrator stared at the narrow staircase, convinced it was impossible.

"Big Daddy, this ain't gonna work," he said, shaking his head.

Big Daddy frowned. "Ain't no such thing as 'can't.' We'll figure it out."

The process was grueling. They had to maneuver the bulky appliance through tight spaces, the narrator's arms burning with the effort. Big Daddy didn't complain or pause for a break—he just kept going, his determination unwavering.

By the time they got the refrigerator upstairs, the narrator was exhausted but proud.

"You see?" Big Daddy said, clapping him on the back. "You're stronger than you think. Remember that."

The Quiet Breakfast

After the work was done, Big Daddy sat the narrator down at the kitchen table. A plate of grits, eggs, and toast awaited him.

"Eat up," Big Daddy said, pouring himself another cup of coffee. "You earned it."

As they ate, Big Daddy shared stories of his youth—tales of hard labor in the South, of sacrifices made to build a life for his family.

"Life ain't easy," he said, his voice steady. "But hard work never killed nobody. Laziness, though? That'll get you every time."

The Unspoken Bond

Though Big Daddy rarely expressed his emotions outright, the narrator felt his love in the little things: the way he showed him how to use tools, the way he insisted on doing things the right way, the way he sat beside him in silence after a long day.

One morning, as they sat on the porch watching the sunrise, Big Daddy spoke quietly.

"You're gonna do great things, boy. I can see it in you. Just don't let the world make you soft."

The narrator nodded, those words sinking deep into his heart.

14
riding with q

*R*iding with Q wasn't just about getting from one place to another—it was a crash course in the complexities of loyalty, survival, and the unspoken rules of the streets. Q was more than a cousin to the narrator; he was a protector, a mentor, and a living example of what it meant to navigate a world where trust was scarce and danger was always around the corner.

The Bass That Shook the Block

The sound of bass booming from Q's car could be heard from three blocks away. The beat seemed to echo off every building, announcing his presence long before he arrived. When Q pulled up, his sleek car glimmered in the sunlight, and the narrator couldn't help but feel a sense of awe.

"Hop in, little cuz," Q called out, his voice smooth and confident.

The narrator slid into the passenger seat, the leather warm from the afternoon sun. The air inside smelled of cologne and cigarette smoke, a combination that somehow felt comforting.

A Ride with Lessons

The streets of Detroit passed by in a blur as Q navigated them with ease. To the narrator, it felt like Q knew every turn, every shortcut, and every story behind each corner.

"Where you headed?" Q asked, glancing at him.

"I was trying to get back to Pops' place," the narrator replied.

Q nodded, turning down the music slightly. "Alright, but first, we gotta make a stop."

They pulled into a corner store, the music still thumping lightly in the background. Q stepped out, leaving the car running.

"Stay here," he said, his tone casual but firm.

The Unexpected Encounter

Minutes later, Q emerged from the store, but something was different. His stride slowed, his posture stiffened. The narrator followed his gaze to a man sitting in a nearby car, his face partially hidden behind tinted windows.

Q walked over to the car, his hand resting casually at his waist. The narrator's heart pounded as he watched the exchange.

"Where my money at?" Q asked, his voice low but laced with authority.

The man hesitated, then reached into his glove compartment. He handed over a wad of cash, his hands shaking slightly.

"That's only half," Q said, stepping back. "Next time, it better be all of it—or you won't like what happens."

Without another word, Q returned to the car, his demeanor calm as if nothing had happened.

"Don't let nobody play you, Rell," Q said as they drove off. "Respect is everything out here, and sometimes you gotta remind people of that."

A Conversation About Loyalty

As they drove, Q turned the music down completely and looked over at the narrator.

"You ever hear about the rules of the streets?" Q asked.

"Not really," the narrator admitted.

"Well, let me tell you something. Out here, it ain't about who's the toughest or the loudest. It's about loyalty. You take care of your people, and they take care of you. But the second somebody crosses you, you gotta handle it."

The narrator nodded, the weight of Q's words settling in.

The Stop at Glenwood

Before dropping him off, Q took a detour through Glenwood, the narrator's old neighborhood. The streets were alive with activity—kids playing, adults chatting on porches, and the occasional dice game happening in the shadows.

"You miss it?" Q asked, his tone more curious than judgmental.

"Sometimes," the narrator replied, watching as familiar faces passed by.

"Well, don't get too comfortable. You got bigger things ahead of you," Q said, his eyes scanning the block.

The Drop-Off

When they finally pulled up to Pops' house, Q turned to the narrator, his expression serious.

"Listen, little cuz. Life ain't gonna hand you nothing. You gotta take it. But you do it smart, you hear me?"

"Yeah, I hear you," the narrator replied, stepping out of the car.

"Good. And if you ever need me, you know where to find me," Q said, giving him a firm handshake before driving off.

As the narrator watched the car disappear down the street, he realized that the ride had been more than a trip through the city—it had been a lesson in survival, loyalty, and the realities of life.

15
fishing with pops and tb

ishing with Pops wasn't just an activity—it was an initiation into a slower, more reflective way of life. Away from the constant noise and movement of the streets, the narrator found himself connecting with nature, his little brother TB, and, most importantly, his father. This outing wasn't about catching fish; it was about catching moments that would stay with him forever.

The Call to Adventure

"Fellas, wrap up whatever you're doing. We're going fishing," Pops announced as he pulled into the driveway, the car engine still humming.

The narrator glanced at TB, who was already smiling wide. TB loved these moments with Pops, and the narrator could sense his excitement.

"Come on, now," Pops said. "Grab the poles and the tackle box. Let's go before it gets too late."

With that, the narrator and TB hurried to the car, tossing their gear into the trunk.

The Journey to the Riverfront

As they drove to the Detroit River, the car filled with the smell of fresh bait and the sound of old-school R&B on Pops' stereo. The narrator leaned back, watching the city transform into open stretches of water and greenery.

"Y'all ever fish before?" Pops asked, glancing at them in the rearview mirror.

TB nodded enthusiastically. "Yeah, Big Daddy took us once, but we didn't catch nothing."

"Well, you're gonna learn today," Pops replied with a grin.

The First Cast

They arrived at the riverfront, a quiet spot where the water lapped gently against the shore. Pops chose a prime spot and handed each of them a fishing rod.

"Here's how it works," Pops said, demonstrating how to bait the hook and cast the line. "You gotta be patient. Fishing ain't about rushing—it's about waiting for the right moment."

The narrator struggled with his first few casts, the line tangling or landing too close to shore. TB, on the other hand, seemed to get the hang of it quickly, casting his line out with a triumphant shout.

"You'll get it," Pops said to the narrator, clapping him on the back. "Just keep at it."

The Quiet Moments

As the hours passed, the world seemed to slow down. The narrator watched the water ripple, the sun reflecting off its surface like shattered glass. Pops sat beside him, his line steady, his eyes focused on the horizon.

"Fishing teaches you a lot about life," Pops said suddenly, breaking the silence. "You can't force things to happen. Sometimes you just gotta wait for what's meant for you."

The narrator nodded, letting the words sink in. It wasn't just a lesson about fishing—it was a lesson about patience, perseverance, and trust.

A Bond Rekindled

TB's excitement broke the calm as he felt a tug on his line. "I got something!" he shouted, reeling in with all his might.

Pops and the narrator rushed over to help, guiding him as he pulled a small perch from the water. TB's smile lit up the entire riverbank, and Pops laughed, clapping him on the back.

"That's my boy!" Pops said, his pride evident.

The narrator felt a twinge of jealousy but quickly pushed it aside. This was their moment, and he was happy to be a part of it.

A Conversation with Pops

As the day wound down and the sky turned shades of orange and pink, the narrator found himself sitting alone with Pops. TB had wandered off to explore the shoreline.

"Son," Pops began, his voice softer now, "I know I haven't always been there for you. But I'm here now, and I want to make up for lost time."

The narrator looked at him, surprised by the vulnerability in his tone. "I know, Pops," he said quietly. "I'm just glad we're getting this time now."

Pops nodded, his eyes fixed on the water. "Me too. You're a good kid, Rell. I see a lot of myself in you. But you're gonna be better than I ever was—I'm sure of it."

Packing Up

As the sun dipped below the horizon, Pops announced it was time to head home. They packed up their gear, leaving the riverfront with empty coolers but full hearts.

"Next time, we'll catch the big ones," Pops said, ruffling TB's hair.

"Yeah, and I'll catch more than both of y'all!" TB replied, his voice brimming with excitement.

The narrator chuckled, watching TB and Pops banter as they loaded the car. For the first time in a long while, the world felt simple, like the weight of everything outside this moment could be paused, if only temporarily.

The Drive Home

The ride back was quieter, the air filled with the hum of the car engine and the distant crackle of the radio. Pops turned the music down, leaning back in his seat with one hand on the wheel.

"Fishing's not always about catching something," he said, his voice carrying the weight of unspoken wisdom. "Sometimes, it's about the time you spend doing it. Remember that."

The narrator nodded, staring out the window at the dimming lights of the city. In the stillness of the car, he realized the significance of what Pops was teaching him—about patience, about presence, and about the value of moments shared with family.

16
the night of the dice game

*B*ack at Pops' house, the nights were anything but quiet. Pops had a reputation for hosting the kind of dice games that drew people from all corners of the neighborhood. For the narrator, this wasn't just another night—it was a glimpse into a world where skill, confidence, and street smarts dictated everything.

The Setup

The living room was transformed into an arena. Pops rearranged the furniture to make room for the table, where the dice would decide the night's fortunes. Plates of food lined the kitchen counter, and beers chilled in the refrigerator. Pops' old-school R&B playlist set the mood, filling the house with a rhythmic energy that promised excitement.

"Rell," Pops called, motioning him over. "You're in charge of the food and drinks tonight. Keep things running smooth, and keep your eyes open. If anything looks off, you let me know."

The narrator nodded, feeling both the weight of responsibility and the thrill of being included in something so significant.

The Players Arrive

By 11:00 p.m., the house was alive with the sounds of laughter, banter, and the clink of dice against wood. The players were a mix of seasoned gamblers and younger men trying to prove themselves. Each carried an air of confidence, their pockets bulging with wads of cash.

"Who's ready to lose their money tonight?" Pops called out, his voice carrying a playful challenge.

The crowd erupted in laughter, and the games began.

The High Stakes

As the night wore on, the stakes grew higher. Pops dominated the table, his skill with the dice matched only by his ability to read people. Every roll was a calculated risk, every bet a test of nerve.

"You see that?" Pops whispered to the narrator, motioning to a player fidgeting in his chair. "That one's bluffing. Watch how he folds when I up the ante."

Sure enough, the man hesitated, his confidence faltering as Pops raised his bet. The narrator watched in awe, realizing that this wasn't just a game—it was a battle of wits and strategy.

A Moment of Tension

The atmosphere shifted when a newcomer, a young man with a brash demeanor, accused Pops of cheating. The room fell silent, all eyes on the two men.

"You calling me a liar?" Pops asked, his voice calm but deadly.

The young man hesitated, the weight of Pops' reputation pressing down on him. Finally, he shook his head. "Nah, I'm just saying... never mind."

Pops leaned back, his gaze never wavering. "Good. 'Cause if you don't trust the table, you don't belong here."

The tension eased, and the games resumed. But the narrator couldn't shake the realization that respect was as much a currency here as the money on the table.

The End of the Night

By 5:00 a.m., the house had emptied, the players leaving with lighter pockets and stories to tell. Pops sat back, counting his winnings with a satisfied grin.

"You did good tonight, son," he said, handing the narrator a stack of bills. "Keep it. You earned it."

The narrator stared at the money, feeling a surge of pride. It wasn't just about the cash—it was about the trust Pops had shown in him.

17

a walk through glenwood

Glenwood wasn't just a neighborhood—it was a world of its own. It was where the narrator first learned the rhythms of the streets, where survival and loyalty went hand in hand. Walking through Glenwood as an older and more experienced version of himself, the narrator saw the neighborhood with new eyes—both as a reflection of his past and as a reminder of how far he'd come.

The Return

The narrator had Pops drop him off at the corner of Kelly and Hayes, just a few blocks from Glenwood. The moment his feet hit the pavement, he felt the familiar pull of the place he once called home. The streets were alive with energy: kids playing tag, old heads sipping from brown paper bags, and music blasting from car stereos.

As he made his way down the block, faces turned to watch him. Some were familiar, others new. It wasn't long before someone called out.

"Yo, Rell! That you, man?"

He turned to see his old friend Jay leaning against a parked car with a cigarette in hand.

"Yeah, it's me," the narrator replied, shaking hands with Jay.

"Damn, it's been a minute," Jay said, grinning. "You still running these streets, or you gone all corporate on us?"

The narrator chuckled, but there was a bittersweetness to Jay's words. Glenwood hadn't changed much, but he had.

The Corner Crew

As he reached the heart of Glenwood, the narrator spotted a group of men shooting dice on the sidewalk. He recognized a few of them from his younger days, their faces older but still carrying the same intensity.

"Rell! Get over here!" one of them shouted.

He hesitated for a moment before walking over. The crew welcomed him back like he'd never left, handing him the dice.

"You still got it?" someone asked, a challenge in their voice.

The narrator rolled, his hands steady. The dice hit the pavement, and the crowd erupted in cheers as he hit his point.

"Still got it," he said with a grin.

A New Perspective

Walking further down the block, the narrator passed the corner store where he used to buy snacks as a kid. It looked the same, but now it felt smaller, less significant.

He thought about the days he spent here, running errands for older guys, learning the rules of the streets. Back then, this block was his entire world. Now, it was a piece of a much larger puzzle.

"Funny how things change," he muttered to himself.

The Encounter

Not everything in Glenwood was a fond memory. As he rounded a corner, he spotted a group of young men dressed in red—clear members of a rival crew.

They noticed him immediately, their eyes narrowing.

"What you doing here, blue boy?" one of them asked, stepping forward.

The narrator felt his pulse quicken, but he stood his ground.

"I grew up here," he said, his voice calm but firm.

"Don't mean you safe now," another one said, smirking.

Before the situation could escalate, a familiar voice rang out.

"Yo, chill! That's Rell—you don't mess with him."

It was P, the neighborhood legend, stepping out from a nearby house. The rival crew exchanged glances before backing off.

"You good?" P asked, walking over to the narrator.

"Yeah, I'm good," the narrator replied, shaking P's hand.

"Keep your head up, man. This place ain't what it used to be," P said before disappearing back into the house.

Reflection

The walk back to Pops' house was quieter, the energy of Glenwood lingering in his mind. The streets had shaped him, taught him lessons that school never could. But they also reminded him of what he was leaving behind—the risks, the rivalries, the constant hustle to stay ahead.

He realized that while Glenwood would always be a part of him, it didn't have to define him.

18
the risky lick

Sometimes, life in the streets demands decisions that teeter on the edge of desperation and survival. For the narrator, "hitting a lick" wasn't just about making money—it was about proving himself, securing respect, and, most importantly, staying one step ahead of the game. This particular lick, however, was different—it was more dangerous, more chaotic, and it would leave an impression he wouldn't soon forget.

The Plan

It started with Blue, one of the narrator's longtime associates, laying out the details on a humid summer night. They were sitting in the backyard of Smoke's crib, the air thick with tension and cigarette smoke.

"This dude keeps flashing money and riding clean through the hood," Blue said, his voice low but urgent. "He ain't one of us, and he's got no business showing out like that. We could take him, easy."

The narrator looked over at Smoke, who was nodding in agreement. Smoke, always quick with a plan and even quicker with a pistol, grinned.

"Rell, we need you," Smoke said. "Just be the lookout. Easy money."

The narrator hesitated. He didn't like the way Blue was hyping it up, but the promise of a quick payday was hard to ignore. After all, $5,000 split between them could go a long way.

The Setup

At 3:00 a.m., the crew assembled outside the target's house. Smoke had his .38 tucked in his waistband, and Blue carried a crowbar. Little TJ, the youngest of the group, was there for backup, though he looked more nervous than ready.

"You sure about this?" the narrator asked Smoke as they crouched behind a bush.

Smoke smirked. "Ain't no sure in this game, cuz. Just do your part, and we'll be straight."

The target's car—a sleek black Cadillac—was parked in the driveway, glinting under the streetlight. The plan was simple: Blue would break in and hotwire the car, Smoke would keep watch on the house, and the narrator would monitor the street for any cops or unexpected interruptions.

The Moment of Action

Blue moved first, sliding up to the car with the crowbar in hand. With practiced ease, he pried the door open and climbed inside. The sound of the car door creaking felt deafening in the stillness of the night, and the narrator's pulse quickened.

From his vantage point on the sidewalk, the narrator scanned the street, his eyes darting between the houses and the road. Everything seemed quiet—until the front door of the house opened.

A man stepped out, his face twisted in confusion as he spotted Blue in the car. Before he could react, Smoke appeared from the shadows, gun in hand.

"Back inside," Smoke growled, his voice low but menacing. The man froze, his hands raised as he backed into the doorway.

"Move, Blue!" Smoke hissed, glancing over his shoulder.

The Cadillac roared to life, its engine cutting through the silence. Blue backed out of the driveway as Smoke ran to the car. The narrator followed, his heart pounding as they sped off into the night.

The Fallout

The adrenaline rush from the successful hit was short-lived. As they pulled into Wayne's chop shop, the reality of what they'd just done began to sink in. Wayne, an older man with a reputation for making stolen cars disappear, greeted them with a knowing smile.

"Nice work, boys," he said, inspecting the Cadillac. "This one's clean. I'll get you your cut in the morning."

The crew laughed and high-fived, but the narrator couldn't shake the uneasy feeling settling in his chest. Smoke handed him $1,250, grinning. "See? Told you it'd be easy."

The money felt heavier than it should have. It wasn't just the risk that weighed on him—it was the realization that one wrong move could have landed them in jail or worse.

The Reflection

Back at Smoke's house, the narrator sat on the porch, staring at the wad of cash in his hands. He thought about Pops, about Big Mama, about the lessons they'd tried to teach him. This wasn't the life they wanted for him—but it was the life he was living.

Smoke joined him, lighting a cigarette. "What's on your mind, Rell?"

"Nothing," the narrator replied, pocketing the money. "Just thinking."

"Well, don't think too hard," Smoke said, exhaling a cloud of smoke. "You did good tonight."

The Risk

The next day, word of the stolen Cadillac spread through the neighborhood. Some people praised the crew's boldness; others warned them to lay low. The narrator avoided the praise, his unease growing with every passing hour.

He knew he'd have to make a choice soon: continue down this path or find a way out before it was too late.

19
smoke's lesson

Smoke was more than just a friend to the narrator—he was a teacher of the streets, an unpredictable figure who balanced charm with danger. His lessons came unfiltered, drawn from a life of survival and raw experience. For the narrator, one of Smoke's lessons stood out as a defining moment—a turning point that challenged his understanding of trust, loyalty, and the consequences of their lifestyle.

The Setup

It was early evening when Smoke called the narrator to his house. The sun was setting, casting long shadows across the block. The narrator walked up to Smoke's porch, where Smoke sat cleaning his .38 revolver, his movements deliberate and precise.

"Cuzo, I got something for you to see," Smoke said, not looking up.

The narrator raised an eyebrow. "What now?"

"Just get inside," Smoke said, his voice calm but carrying a tone that left no room for argument.

Inside the house, Smoke led the narrator to the kitchen. On the counter sat a glass jar, a box of baking soda, and a small bag of white powder. The air felt heavier, charged with an intensity that made the narrator's stomach tighten.

"You know what this is?" Smoke asked, tapping the jar.

"Yeah, it's coke," the narrator replied, his voice cautious.

"Nah," Smoke said with a grin. "It's opportunity."

The Process

Smoke began demonstrating how to cook crack cocaine, walking the narrator through each step with a level of focus that bordered on obsession.

"First, you boil the water," he said, turning on the stove. "Then you add this—just enough to liquefy it. Once it's smooth, you hit it with the baking soda."

The narrator watched as Smoke worked, his movements methodical. The liquid in the jar began to transform, hardening into a crystalline substance.

"This," Smoke said, holding up the finished product, "is what keeps the money coming. It's what keeps people in line. You get this right, and you'll never be broke again."

The First Sale

Smoke handed the narrator a small bag of the finished product. "Now, let's see if you can move it," he said.

The narrator hesitated, the weight of the bag feeling disproportionate to its size. "I don't know, man. This ain't me."

Smoke laughed, shaking his head. "Ain't you? What you think you been doing all this time? Hustling is hustling, Rell. Don't overthink it. Just get out there and make it happen."

Against his better judgment, the narrator took the bag. He knew Smoke wouldn't let him walk away without trying, and deep down, he was curious.

The Streets' Response

The first few sales were easier than the narrator expected. People approached him with cash in hand, their desperation palpable. Within an hour, he was sold out, his pockets heavier with cash than they'd ever been.

When he returned to Smoke's house, Smoke greeted him with a proud grin. "See? I told you. Easy money."

But the narrator didn't feel proud. The looks on the faces of the people he'd sold to lingered in his mind—haunted, hollow, broken.

"This ain't right," the narrator said, handing the cash to Smoke.

"Right or wrong don't matter out here," Smoke replied, pocketing the money. "All that matters is getting yours before somebody else does."

A Moment of Doubt

That night, the narrator sat on his porch, staring at the stars. He thought about Pops, Big Mama, and the values they'd tried to instill in him. He thought about the people he'd sold to, their lives unraveling one hit at a time.

Smoke joined him, lighting a cigarette.

"You're thinking too much again," Smoke said, exhaling a plume of smoke.

"Maybe you're not thinking enough," the narrator shot back.

Smoke chuckled. "That's why we balance each other out, cuz. You keep me grounded, and I keep you moving."

The narrator didn't respond. For the first time, he wondered if their paths were diverging in ways neither of them fully understood.

The Unspoken Bond

Despite their differences, Smoke and the narrator shared an unbreakable bond. Smoke was the brother he didn't choose but couldn't imagine life without. And even though they didn't always agree, there was a loyalty between them that neither questioned.

"You're good at this, Rell," Smoke said quietly. "Better than you want to admit. But you gotta decide for yourself if you're gonna use it or not."

The narrator nodded, the weight of the decision pressing down on him.

20
crossing the line

The line between survival and destruction in the streets is razor-thin, and the narrator found himself walking it with increasing frequency. In this chapter, the stakes rise, and a moment of impulsive action forces him to confront the consequences of living in a world where respect and power are earned through risk.

The Decision

It started with a phone call late at night. Smoke's voice came through the line, low and urgent.

"Yo, Rell. We got a problem," he said.

"What kind of problem?" the narrator asked, already dreading the answer.

"Blue ran his mouth to the wrong people," Smoke explained. "Now they think we soft. We gotta remind them who they're dealing with."

The narrator hesitated. He knew what Smoke meant, and he wasn't sure he wanted to be part of it.

"Man, I don't know," he said.

"Don't think too hard, cuz," Smoke replied. "Just meet me at the spot. We need you on this."

The Setup

The spot was an abandoned warehouse on the edge of the neighborhood. When the narrator arrived, Smoke and a few others were already there, their faces grim. On the table lay a pistol and a wad of cash.

"What's the plan?" the narrator asked, his voice steady despite the tension in the room.

"We're gonna hit their stash house," Smoke said. "Show them they can't mess with us."

The narrator's stomach tightened. This wasn't just about money or reputation—it was about sending a message. And messages in the streets were written in blood.

The Execution

The drive to the stash house was silent, the weight of the moment pressing down on everyone in the car. Smoke parked a block away, cutting the engine.

"Rell, you're with me," Smoke said, handing him the pistol.

The narrator took it reluctantly, the cold metal heavy in his hand. He followed Smoke down the alley, his heart pounding as they approached the back door of the house.

Smoke kicked the door open, the sound echoing through the empty streets. Inside, the air was thick with tension. Three men sat around a table, their eyes wide with shock as Smoke raised his gun.

"Hands up!" Smoke barked.

The narrator kept his weapon trained on the group, his hands trembling. One of the men reached for something under the table, and without thinking, the narrator fired.

The sound of the gunshot was deafening, and for a moment, everything froze. The man slumped forward, blood pooling beneath him.

"Shit!" Smoke shouted, pulling the narrator back toward the door. "Let's go!"

The Aftermath

Back at Smoke's house, the atmosphere was tense. The crew counted the cash and drugs they'd taken, but the narrator couldn't focus. His hands were still shaking, and his mind replayed the moment over and over.

"You did what you had to do," Smoke said, clapping him on the shoulder.

"Did I?" the narrator asked, his voice barely above a whisper.

Smoke nodded. "Out here, it's kill or be killed. You did right."

But the narrator wasn't convinced. He felt a weight settle on his chest—a mix of guilt, fear, and anger at himself for crossing a line he hadn't even realized existed.

A Conversation with Pops

That night, the narrator sat on Pops' porch, unable to sleep. Pops joined him, a cigarette in hand.

"You look like you got the weight of the world on your shoulders," Pops said, exhaling a cloud of smoke.

"I messed up," the narrator admitted.

Pops studied him for a moment before speaking. "Ain't nobody out here perfect, son. But you gotta decide what kind of man you wanna be. The streets will take everything from you if you let them. Don't let them."

The Turning Point

The narrator's mind raced with Pops' words as he sat alone later that night. He realized he couldn't keep living like this, letting the streets dictate his every move. But walking away wasn't simple. Loyalty to Smoke and the crew pulled him in one direction, while his growing desire for something more pulled him in another.

He knew one thing for sure—he couldn't keep crossing lines without losing himself completely.

21
a moment of clarity

In the chaos of the streets, moments of clarity can feel like lifelines. For the narrator, the weight of his recent choices had been building, each decision pulling him further from the person he wanted to be. But clarity rarely comes without pain, and this moment was no exception. It was a turning point, one that forced him to confront his life, his loyalty, and the future he truly wanted.

The Restless Night

Sleep wouldn't come. The events of the stash house replayed in the narrator's mind like a broken record, each frame sharper and more vivid than the last. The sound of the gunshot, the look in the man's eyes—it all haunted him.

He paced his room, the cash from the hit still sitting on the dresser. It should have felt like a victory, but it didn't. Instead, it felt like a chain, binding him further to a life he was no longer sure he wanted.

The faint sound of Pops' favorite oldies playing from the living room broke through his thoughts. Unable to stay in the confines of his room any longer, the narrator made his way downstairs.

The Porch Conversation

Pops was sitting on the porch, a cigarette in one hand and a glass of whiskey in the other. He didn't say anything when the narrator joined him, simply gesturing toward the empty chair beside him.

For a while, they sat in silence; the city sounds filling the space between them. Finally, Pops spoke.

"You ever feel like the world's spinning faster than you can keep up?" Pops asked, staring out into the street.

"Yeah," the narrator replied, his voice low. "All the time."

Pops nodded, taking a long drag of his cigarette. "That's life, son. But you gotta find your center. If you don't, you'll get spun out and thrown off course."

A Visit to Big Mama

The next morning, the narrator decided to visit Big Mama. Her house was always a sanctuary, a place where the weight of the streets seemed to lift, even if only temporarily.

When he arrived, she was in the garden, tending to her collard greens. She looked up and smiled as he approached.

"Baby, you look like you've been carrying the world on your shoulders," she said, wiping her hands on her apron. "Come sit with me."

As they sat on the porch, Big Mama spoke about resilience and faith, about how the world would test you but never give you more than you could handle.

"You're stronger than you think," she said, her voice steady. "But you gotta decide what you're fighting for. You can't win every battle, but you can choose the ones worth fighting."

The Decision

That evening, the narrator found himself back on the block, watching the familiar rhythm of the streets. Smoke was there, laughing and joking with the crew like nothing had happened. But to the narrator, everything felt different.

He approached Smoke, his resolve hardening with each step.

"Cuzo, I think I'm done," he said, his voice steady.

Smoke frowned, his laughter fading. "What you mean, done?"

"I mean this life. I can't do it anymore."

Smoke studied him for a long moment, then nodded slowly. "Alright. But just know once you're out, you're out. Ain't no coming back."

The narrator nodded. "I know."

The First Steps Forward

Walking away wasn't easy. The streets didn't let go without a fight, and the narrator knew he'd have to prove himself in a different way now. But for the first time in years, he felt a sense of freedom, a glimmer of hope for a future that didn't feel shackled by the past.

He spent more time with Pops, learning from his wisdom, and with Big Mama, soaking in her resilience. He started to see the world beyond the block, recognizing the possibilities he'd once ignored.

22

tornado on hickory street

*H*ickory Street always felt alive, like it had its own pulse. The houses sat in neat rows, a mix of older brick homes and wooden structures weathered by the passing years. Kids played on porches, neighbors called out to each other, and there was always the distant hum of a car stereo booming down the block. It wasn't perfect, but it was home.

That day started like any other. Your mom was in the kitchen, humming softly as she prepared lunch. The scent of frying bologna filled the air, mingling with the faint smell of rain that had started hours earlier. You sat at the window, staring out at the street. The clouds overhead were thick and gray, the kind that made the world feel smaller.

"I'm going to Jeff's," you called out, grabbing your bike from the hallway.

Your mom glanced over her shoulder, her brow furrowed slightly. She had a way of sensing things, like the weather wasn't the only storm brewing. "Don't be out too long. It's looking bad out there," she warned, her voice firm.

You shrugged it off. "I'll be fine," you said, pushing open the screen door.

The ride to Jeff's was quick. The two of you had been best friends for as long as you could remember. His house, just one block over, felt like an extension of your own. As you pedaled down the street, you nodded to Mrs. Green, the elderly woman who always sat on her porch. She waved back, her hand trembling slightly from age.

But as you turned the corner onto Jeff's block, the air shifted. It wasn't just the wind picking up—it was the way the entire street seemed to hold its breath. The laughter of kids playing hopscotch faded. A dog barked once, then fell silent. Even the usual hum of car engines seemed to vanish.

When you reached Jeff's house, he was already standing on the porch, his arms crossed. Jeff was a wiry kid with a mop of curly hair that always seemed to stick out in every direction. His face was lit with excitement, but there was a nervous energy behind his smile.

"Man, look at that sky," he said, pointing toward the horizon.

You followed his gaze and felt your stomach drop. The clouds weren't just dark—they were alive. They twisted and churned, forming ominous spirals that seemed to reach down toward the earth. You'd never seen anything like it.

"I think I should head back," you said, your voice shaking slightly.

Jeff nodded. "Yeah, you probably should. My mom's been talking about tornado warnings all morning."

Tornado warnings. The words hit you like a punch to the gut. You'd heard about them on TV, seen the destruction they could cause, but it always felt like something distant, something that happened somewhere else. Not here.

Without another word, you jumped on your bike and took off. The wind pushed against you, stronger now, as if trying to keep you from getting home. The rain started as a drizzle but quickly turned into a downpour, soaking through your clothes.

And then it happened.

The sky turned black, an unnatural darkness that made it impossible to see more than a few feet ahead. The wind screamed in your ears, loud and relentless. Trash cans rolled down the street, their lids clattering like cymbals. A tree branch snapped and crashed onto the pavement just feet away from you.

Panic set in. Your heart raced as you jumped off your bike and started running. Your legs burned, but you didn't stop. You couldn't. The sound of the wind was deafening now, drowning out your thoughts.

"God, please let me make it home," you whispered, the words spilling out of you like a prayer. You weren't even sure where they came from—it was instinct, pure and desperate.

Finally, through the sheets of rain and swirling debris, you saw it: your house. The porch light was on, casting a warm glow that cut through the chaos. It felt like a lifeline, pulling you forward.

You stumbled up the steps, nearly tripping as you reached for the door. It flew open before you could touch it, and there she was—your mom. Her eyes were wide with fear, her arms outstretched. She pulled you inside, slamming the door shut behind you.

"What were you thinking?" she yelled, her voice trembling. "I told you to stay close!"

You couldn't answer. You were too busy gasping for air, your chest heaving as you tried to catch your breath. Your clothes were soaked, your shoes caked in mud.

But then her anger softened. She knelt down, her hands gripping your shoulders, and looked you in the eyes. "Are you okay?" she asked, her voice quieter now, almost breaking.

You nodded, tears welling up despite yourself.

She pulled you into a tight hug, holding you as if her arms could shield you from everything that had just happened. "Thank God you're safe," she whispered.

As you sat there in her embrace, the storm raged on outside. The windows rattled, the wind howled, but inside, you felt a strange sense of calm. It wasn't just the relief of being home—it was the realization that, no matter how chaotic the world became, you had someone who would always be there to protect you.

That day wasn't just about surviving a tornado. It was about understanding the strength of the people around you and the fragility of life itself. It was a lesson you didn't fully grasp at the time but would carry with you forever.

23

the price of survival

$\mathcal{A}$s I dove deeper into the streets, I witnessed the true cost of survival. The violence, the lies, the backstabbing—all of it came with a price. At 15, I saw my first glimpse of death. A cop got killed, and the news spread like wildfire. It wasn't the first time I'd seen bloodshed, but something about it shook me to the core. I knew I had to make a choice—keep living this life or find a way out.

But getting out wasn't easy. The streets had a way of pulling you back in. I remember the time when I had a run-in with a guy who thought he could push me around. A black-skinned dude, smooth in his approach, tried to run me off the block. But Smoke was there, stepping in like a true mentor. "Tywan, baby, chill out. That's my brother, Cuzo's nephew. He's good," Smoke said. And just like that, the situation was diffused. It was moments like that that showed me the value of loyalty and respect in this game.

I remember how the game would draw you in, no matter how hard you tried to stay out. You could feel it in the air, the pressure building up as more people came around. I loved the dice games, especially 456. I used to play as the banker, making big money in those games. But I wasn't just in it for the money; I was in it to stay connected, to keep my status, and to keep people from thinking I was weak.

24

childhood roots and survival

Growing up in the heart of Detroit, survival was the first lesson I learned. The world around me wasn't forgiving, and the streets offered no mercy. From the start, I had to fight for everything—whether it was respect, money, or just getting through another day. My childhood was filled with chaos, but it also planted the seeds for who I would become.

I was just a kid, riding my bike with friends, when life threw its first curveball. A car sped down the street and hit my best friend's cousin. The block froze in fear and confusion. The driver fled, chaos unfolded, and people scrambled to help. I watched it all happen, but I wasn't surprised—this was life on the Eastside. It was a harsh reality where you had to keep your head on a swivel and stay ready for whatever came next.

Later that night, I was sitting on the porch of Pops' house. Pops had been a steady force in my life, a reminder that there was a different way to move in this world. I'd spent too many nights out, losing track of time, but that night was different. He came outside, his voice sharp with concern.

"Where the hell you been, boy?" he asked, his voice filled with both worry and authority. "If you're gonna live under my roof, you need to follow some rules. I don't care how you lived before, but in this house, there's order."

Pops was a man of few words, but when he spoke, you listened. He wanted to make sure I was grounded, that I didn't get lost in the streets. The smell of goulash cooking in the kitchen filled the air, and the sounds of Bruce Lee's *Enter the Dragon* echoed in the background, his favorite movie. I didn't fully understand it at the time, but Pops was trying to teach me something deeper—about discipline, respect, and the importance of family.

25

lessons from the streets

*A*s I got older, the streets became a school in their own right. I was drawn into the hustle early on, learning from the people around me who had mastered the game. Smoke, a mentor in my life, taught me the ropes. He showed me how to move through the world with a quiet confidence, how to handle pressure, and how to turn nothing into something. It wasn't just about money—it was about survival.

"Man, whatever Smoke did when he wiped this shit up, they love it. It was car after car pulling up," I remember thinking. The game wasn't always easy, but it was how I made a living. I remember times when I'd find myself caught up in the moment, about to make a decision that could change everything. But I always knew one thing: if you didn't stay alert, you'd get left behind.

I had people like Ronnie D who would pull up on me with business. "Man, don't get nothing else. This shit is it. Let me get $300," he said one day. The hustle was real, and I was right in the thick of it. But it wasn't all about the money. I was learning lessons I couldn't have gotten anywhere else. I was learning how to survive, how to move with caution, and how to make sure that my word was always solid.

26

turning point – music as salvation

While I was building my reputation in the streets, I knew that I couldn't keep living this way forever. I wanted something different. Music had always been a part of me, a way to express what I was going through, but it wasn't until later that I realized its true power. Music could change lives. It could give people a way out, a way to escape the harsh reality of their surroundings.

That's when I started thinking about *World of Music*. I wanted to create a space where kids, especially those from tough backgrounds like mine, could come and find something that could lift them up. I wanted them to know that there was more to life than the streets. I wanted them to know that they didn't have to follow in my footsteps.

I began working with underprivileged youth, showing them the value of music, of creativity, and of hard work. I knew it wouldn't be easy, but I was determined to make it happen. This was my way of breaking the cycle, of showing these kids that they didn't have to fall into the same traps I did.

World of Music became my way of fighting back—not just for myself, but for the kids I was helping. It wasn't just a program; it was a mission. And with every life I touched, I knew I was making a difference.

27
the fight for my family

But even as I built this program, something was missing. My children—Imani, Pepper, and Terrell Jr.—had been taken from me, and every day without them felt like a piece of me was missing. I fought for them, doing everything I could to get them back, working jobs, building a stable life, and showing the courts that I was ready to be the father they needed.

I worked hard, building two vehicles, two bank accounts, and making sure each of my children had their own room with brand new furniture. I fought tooth and nail, hoping and praying the courts would see that I was more than capable of providing for them. But despite my efforts, the courts refused to return them to me, citing distance from their grandmother. The pain was real, but I kept pushing forward.

28

from novara street to nottingham – the rise of casino cuz'o

Seventeen years old. **Novara Street, Detroit.**

Detroit wasn't just a city; it was a furnace. It molded you, reshaped you, and burned away anything weak until only steel remained. By the time I was seventeen, the streets had already given me a lifetime's worth of lessons—each one paid for in sweat, tears, and blood.

Navarra Street wasn't just where I lived; it was a raw, unforgiving chapter of my life. The cracked sidewalks, the busted streetlights, the smell of liquor and gunpowder hanging in the air—it wasn't chaos to me, it was home. The kind of home where silence wasn't peace; it was danger.

Inside our house, the silence was even louder. My mom wasn't around much. Her absence wasn't something we talked about; it was just something we felt—a dull ache in the walls, in the floors, in the empty spaces where her love should've been.

So, it was me, my brother Shawn, my cousin Tywan, my childhood brother D.C., my cousin Covey, and a couple of their close friends. A house full of young men trying to fill the silence with our own noise, trying to make sense of a world that didn't care if we lived or died.

That house wasn't warm. It wasn't comfortable. The paint peeled off the walls like it was trying to escape. Some nights, the power was cut, and the shadows wrapped around us like suffocating hands. Winters were brutal—we layered ourselves in whatever clothes we could find and huddled for warmth like survivors in a war zone.

The bathroom didn't work half the time, and we'd carry five-gallon buckets of water up and down the stairs just to flush the toilet. Hunger was a shadow that followed us everywhere, sitting in our stomachs and whispering in our ears late at night.

But even in the struggle, there were moments—small, fleeting moments—where we felt untouchable.

One summer day, Willie Will came by the house. He was fifteen, younger than me, but already carrying a weight on his shoulders that most grown men would crumble under. Willie wasn't just a friend; he was family.

That day, he walked in and caught me mid-verse, rapping to a beat spilling out of some busted speakers. The room wasn't just filled with sound—it was filled with *me*. Every bar carried hunger, every rhyme carried survival, every syllable was sharp enough to cut glass.

When I finished, Willie was still. His eyes were wide, his mouth slightly open.

"Yo, Cuz'o… I didn't know you could spit like that!"

His excitement hit me hard. It wasn't just admiration; it was belief.

He told me about a rap group he was part of called the Nutty Boys, and he insisted I meet them. There was no hesitation on my part—I was ready.

When we arrived, standing at the center of the group was Nutcracker—my older cousin. Life has a way of placing you exactly where you need to be, even if you don't recognize it at the moment.

Nutcracker gave me that look—the one older cousins give when they're testing you, seeing if you've got the guts to stand tall.

"Spit something."

I didn't think. I didn't hesitate. I let every word fly like bullets from a chamber. Each line carried my story—the cold nights, the hunger pains, the loneliness of a motherless house, the tightrope walk of survival on streets where one mistake could be your last.

When I finished, there was silence. Then, slowly, heads began to nod. Nutcracker smirked and gave me a nod of approval.

That was it. I was in.

The Nutty Boys weren't just a rap group—they were a family. It was me, Willie Will, Nutcracker, What's-His-Name, and Trey. Together, we weren't just making music—we were carving our names into the concrete of Detroit.

But Detroit doesn't care about brotherhood. The city doesn't care about your dreams, your loyalty, or your hunger.

The conditions we lived in were a war zone. Some days, the lights wouldn't come on. Some nights, we slept fully dressed, not because we were cold, but because we had to be ready to run if gunshots rang out.

But we had our moments—golden moments—where time seemed to freeze. One night, we were out on Loretto Street—me, Willie Will, Nutcracker, and about eight others. We laughed so hard it felt like our ribs would crack. For that night, we weren't poor, we weren't hungry, we weren't scared—we were just kids.

The next day, I went to work at Joe Louis Arena. The Red Wings had just won the Stanley Cup, and the city was electric with pride. I worked in the VIP section, serving millionaires, shaking hands with legends like Chris Chelios, Draper, and Darren McCarty.

For a few hours, I existed in a world so far removed from Navarra Street that it felt like a dream.

But when my shift ended around 4:35 a.m., reality came crashing back.

Willie Will was dead.

I can still hear the echoes of his laugh from Loretto Street. I can still see his face frozen in time. Death has a way of making everything else feel small, insignificant.

Willie's death broke us. The Nutty Boys scattered. The crew was gone.

I ended up on Nottingham Street, trying to rebuild from scratch. I started my own hustle, made my own moves, and started stacking my money. For a brief moment, it felt like I was winning.

Then came Minnesota—a fresh start, a bigger hustle. But the streets are sticky, and I couldn't escape them. I was arrested for first-degree possession and sales and sentenced to four and a half years in prison.

Prison is designed to break men. It's designed to strip you of your dignity and bury your hope six feet under. But I didn't let it. I earned my GED, stayed focused, and made a promise to myself: *if I ever got out, I'd never waste another second.*

When I was released, I faced 18 months of boot camp and 10 years of probation. I completed every step, every condition, without a single violation.

During that time, I met Pepper—the love of my life.

Together, we had three beautiful children:

- Imani Lee Grier
- Pepper Shamus Grier
- Terrell Lavelle Grier Jr.

For 13 years, Pepper and I built something real. But fate struck again. Pepper developed sepsis during experimental treatment while pregnant. Two weeks before she passed away, St. Louis County stripped us of custody of our children. In two weeks, I lost my wife, my unborn child, and my three kids. I spiraled into darkness for four and a half years. But music found me again.

I became Casino Cuz'o, leaving *Cuz'o Nephew* behind. I built:

- World of Music
- A mobile detailing business
- Mind Body Sole
- Casino Cuz'o Apparel Today, I'm not just surviving—I'm thriving.
- And, through it all, I got my criminal record expunged.

I'm building a legacy that will outlive me. I'm showing my kids, my community, and the world that no matter how dark life gets, there's always a way back to the light.

This isn't the end of my story—it's just the beginning.

Reflections in the Rearview

The hum of the highway had always been a comfort, a steady rhythm in the chaos of life. The reflection of streetlights danced across the windshield as I gripped the steering wheel, the weight of countless memories pressing against my chest. Each mile felt like flipping through the pages of a photo album—faces, places, and moments that had carved themselves into my soul.

Life had never been simple, but I had always found a way to make it mine. From the cracked streets of Detroit to the polished floors of corporate buildings where I once built airplanes, every step was a testament to resilience. But it wasn't the victories that lingered in my mind tonight—it was the losses, the close calls, and the echoes of laughter from people who were no longer here.

I thought about Sean, my big brother, standing firm against twenty gang members on Hickory Street. I could still hear the sharp crack of my mom's AK-47 firing into the sky, a sound that cut through the night and told the world: *We don't back down*. That night wasn't just about survival; it was about defiance. About drawing a line in the sand and daring anyone to cross it.

Then there was Jeff's tornado story, the day the sky went dark, and I realized just how small and fragile we all are. I had been just a kid, racing home on my bike, feeling like the storm was chasing me down. But that wasn't the last storm I would face—not by a long shot.

I let out a heavy sigh, my hand absentmindedly tracing the scar on the side of my head, the one from the car accident after leaving Denby High School. Fourteen stitches had held me together, but no needle or thread could ever fully repair the way that moment altered me. It was like life had decided to leave a physical mark to remind me: *You're still here. You're still breathing. Keep going.*

But tonight, the silence of the road brought me back to my children. Imani, Pepper, and Terrell. Their names were etched into every heartbeat, every breath I took. I thought about cutting their umbilical cords, holding them for the first time, and doing my daughter's hair every single morning before school. Those quiet moments were everything to me—small pockets of peace in a life that often felt like a war zone.

The pain of their absence still cut deep. I had fought with everything I had to bring them home, to show the courts, the system, and anyone who doubted me that I was a father worth fighting for. I had built a stable home, worked hard jobs, and ensured they had everything they needed. Yet, the doors to them remained locked. But I wasn't done fighting—not then, not now.

I turned the music up slightly, letting the bass shake the car as I thought about the days spent hustling dice games in schoolyards, risking it all with every roll. *456* wasn't just a game to me—it was survival. And the people I beat back then? Some of them still wanted their money to this day. But those risks weren't just about money; they were about proving something to myself, to the world. *I could win. I would win.*

The past had shaped me, but it wasn't done teaching me yet. Every hardship, every scar, every moment of joy—it had all built the person sitting behind this wheel tonight. And as I looked out at the endless stretch of road ahead, I realized something: the journey wasn't over. There were still chapters left to write, battles left to fight, and love left to give.

I adjusted the rearview mirror and stared at my own reflection for a long moment.

"You made it this far," I whispered to myself. *"Don't stop now."*

The engine roared as I pressed down on the gas, the road stretching out before me like a blank page, waiting to be filled with the next chapter of my story.

29

the weight of loyalty

The glow of the dashboard lights illuminated my face as the miles blurred into a haze. Memories had a way of creeping in during moments like this—when the world was quiet, and it was just me, the road, and my thoughts. Some memories carried warmth, others carried weight, and a few… well, they were heavy enough to crush a man if he wasn't built for it.

One face in particular came to mind as the tires hummed against the asphalt: Tywan, my cousin. He wasn't just family; he was someone who had been in the trenches with me more times than I could count. We had our own language, built from years of shared risks and unspoken loyalty. It wasn't just about blood—it was about trust.

I remembered one night back on Hickory Street, the air thick with tension after Sean stood his ground against the 7 Mile Bloods. It wasn't over after my mom fired those warning shots. When the sun rose, the consequences lingered like smoke after a gunfight. Tywan and I had spent the next few days watching our backs, staying sharp, and making sure Sean wasn't caught slipping. Loyalty wasn't just a word in our circle—it was everything.

But loyalty came with weight. And sometimes, that weight was heavier than any bag of money or trunk full of product.

I thought about DC, too. Another brother in every sense of the word. We were inseparable back then, like shadows attached to one another. Wherever trouble was brewing, we were usually standing nearby, deciding whether to pour gasoline on the fire or walk away. More often than not, we chose fire.

But it wasn't all chaos. Those were the same years we laughed until our stomachs hurt, rolled dice until the sun came up, and shared dreams about getting out. *Out of the hood, out of the cycle, out of the struggle.* We all wanted more, but wanting wasn't enough. You had to bleed for it, fight for it, and sometimes… lose for it.

The streetlights blurred as my thoughts drifted to one of the hardest days of my life: my best friend losing his life at just 15 years old. I could still hear the crack of the gunfire, feel the air leave my lungs when I realized he was gone. That kind of loss stays with you—it lives in your bones. I went to over 15 funerals as a teenager, each one a fresh wound on a heart that was already stitched together with scars.

But it wasn't just the losses that hurt—it was the survivor's guilt. Why them and not me? I had been in the same places, taken the same risks, stood on the same corners. I had been shot over six times, and I was still here. Why?

Maybe it was because I still had work to do. Maybe God had a plan for me that I couldn't see yet.

I gripped the steering wheel tighter, my knuckles turning white as I swallowed back the lump rising in my throat. This life—it wasn't easy, but it was mine. Every scar, every loss, every moment of joy, they were all stitched into the fabric of who I was.

The rearview mirror caught my eyes again, and for a moment, I didn't recognize the man staring back at me. I had been through so much, but I was still standing.

"They tried to break me," I said to no one in particular, my voice steady despite the storm inside me. *"But I'm still here."*

I reached over to turn up the music, letting the beat vibrate through my chest. My mind drifted to the World of Music program, something I had poured my heart into. The same streets that took so much from me had also given me a story—a story I could share with the next generation. Through music, through words, through showing up for kids who felt like nobody was ever going to show up for them.

This wasn't just about survival anymore. It was about legacy. About breaking cycles and building something that would outlive me.

As the road stretched endlessly ahead of me, I made a silent promise—to my kids, to my fallen brothers, and to myself.

"I'm not done yet."

The weight of loyalty, love, and loss sat heavy on my shoulders, but it no longer felt like a burden. It felt like fuel.

And with every mile I drove, I knew one thing for certain: the story wasn't over yet.

30

blood, dice, and survival

The smell of gasoline and burnt rubber still lingered in my memory, sharp and acrid, like the streets I grew up on. Nights under flickering streetlights, the sound of dice clattering against the pavement, and the chorus of voices rising in frustration or celebration—it was all still there, alive in the back of my mind. I wasn't just some kid hanging out on corners; I was a *banker* in the dice game. And being the banker wasn't just about holding money—it was about control.

In the game of 456, control was everything. The dice weren't just cubes—they were fate. Rolling them wasn't about luck; it was about confidence, about reading people, about knowing when to press forward and when to hold back. I had mastered that art young, and it showed. There were nights I walked away with more money than some grown men made in a month. But there were also nights when the wrong roll made everything go sideways.

I remember one night vividly—it was behind the liquor store on Gratiot, just a block down from *Time to Shine*, my uncle Mike's car wash. The air was thick with cigarette smoke and tension. Wads of cash were exchanged, curses were muttered, and the dice hit the ground like gunshots. I was the youngest in the circle, barely sixteen, but I wasn't just another face in the crowd. I was *the* banker, and that meant all eyes were on me.

"Roll 'em, lil' man," one of the older guys said, his gold teeth glinting in the dim light.

I felt the weight of the dice in my palm—cool, heavy, and full of possibility. I closed my eyes for half a second, whispered a prayer I wasn't sure God was even listening to, and let the dice fly.

Four. Five. Six.

The crowd erupted. Money was snatched out of hands, bills were waved in the air, and someone pounded a fist against the brick wall in frustration. I stayed cool, calm, collected. That was the thing about being a young hustler—you couldn't let them see you sweat, no matter how high the stakes were.

But the thing about dice games? They attract wolves. People who were desperate, angry, or just plain reckless. And on nights like this, you could feel it in the air—trouble brewing like a storm on the horizon.

"Run it back!" someone shouted.

But I had a rule: Never push your luck when the air turns sour.

I nodded at Tywan, gave him the signal, and we started collecting. The crowd was too loud and too aggressive, and the vibe was shifting from excitement to danger. I could feel it in my bones.

"Yo, where you goin'?" one guy asked, stepping forward, his shoulders squared up like he wanted to test me.

"We done here," I said, my voice steady, my eyes locked on his.

But he wasn't hearing it. His hand was already reaching under his oversized hoodie, and I knew what was coming.

Fight or flight.

Before I could even think, a car screeched into the lot, headlights cutting through the dark like spotlights on a stage. It was Sean, my brother, with the passenger door flung wide open.

"Get in!" he yelled.

Tywan and I didn't hesitate. We bolted toward the car, the sound of a gunshot cracking behind us as we dove into the backseat. The tires squealed, smoke rose from the pavement, and the car rocketed out of the lot, leaving chaos behind.

My heart was pounding so hard I could feel it in my throat. Tywan was gasping for breath next to me, his hand clutching a stack of cash like it was his lifeline.

Sean glanced at me through the rearview mirror. "Y'all gotta stop playin' dice in spots like that. One day, you ain't gonna make it out."

He was right. But at that moment, all I could think about was how close death had been.

That wasn't the first close call, and it wouldn't be the last. The streets had rules, but they were unwritten, and breaking them didn't always come with warnings. Sometimes, the penalty was instant and final.

When I think back to those nights, it's not the money I remember most—it's the *feeling*. The rush of the gamble, the weight of survival, the unspoken understanding that every roll of the dice could be your last.

But here's the thing: it wasn't just about dice. It was about control. In a world that felt uncontrollable, where poverty, violence, and loss were constants, those dice gave me something I could hold onto. Something I could command.

But the danger, the risks—they weren't sustainable. And deep down, I knew it.

Every time I counted stacks of crumpled bills in the dark or tucked a wad of cash under my mattress, I wondered: *How long can I keep this up before it all falls apart?*

The road ahead wasn't clear, but one thing was certain: I wasn't going back to square one. Not after everything I'd survived.

I leaned my head back against the seat, the sounds of the city fading into the background as Sean drove us away from the chaos. My fists unclenched, and for the first time that night, I allowed myself to exhale.

31
lessons in loyalty and loss

The weight of survival was something I had carried for as long as I could remember. But loyalty? Loyalty was heavier. It wasn't just about standing by someone—it was about being willing to bleed for them, to sacrifice, to make choices that could cost you everything. And sometimes, no matter how loyal you were, life would still find a way to snatch people from you.

I was 15 years old when I lost my best friend.

We had been inseparable since we were kids—two knuckleheads who had each other's backs no matter what. We laughed together, fought together, and dreamed together. Back then, our world was small, but our dreams were big. We wanted better—better than the streets, better than the constant cloud of danger hanging over us, better than the funerals we were growing too familiar with.

But dreams didn't stop bullets.

That day started out like any other. The sun was out, the streets were alive with noise, and the air carried the smell of summer heat baking the concrete. We were supposed to meet up later that night, maybe shoot dice or find a party to crash. But he never made it.

The news hit me like a sledgehammer to the chest. He was gone. Just like that.

I remember standing on the sidewalk, staring at the spot where it happened. The blood had already started to dry, leaving behind a dark stain on the pavement. People were gathered around, whispering, shaking their heads, but I couldn't hear them. All I could hear was this deafening silence in my head, like the world had hit pause.

"Why him?" I kept asking myself. *"Why not me?"*

We had been in the same places, done the same things. It could've been me lying there just as easily. Survivor's guilt—it's a real thing, and it eats at you in the quiet moments. It makes you question every decision, every step you've taken, and every breath you still get to take.

I went to his funeral, but I don't remember much of it. Funerals started to blur together after a while. Fifteen funerals by the time I was 18. Each one chipping away at whatever innocence I had left, replacing it with something colder, something harder.

But here's the thing about loss—it teaches you. It teaches you about loyalty, about the people who show up for you, and about the people who disappear when things get real.

After he died, I started moving differently. I wasn't just surviving anymore—I was *studying*. Watching people, learning their tells, their habits, their weaknesses. The streets weren't forgiving, and being naïve would get you buried next to your best friend.

I threw myself deeper into the hustle—dice games, car deals, anything that could flip money fast. I wasn't just playing to win; I was playing to survive. But even in that chaos, I couldn't stop thinking about him. His laughter, his voice, the way he always said, *"We're gonna make it out, bro."*

But he didn't. And I had to live with that.

One night, a few months after his funeral, I found myself standing outside my cream Chevy Caprice, staring at the car that had become my escape. I had poured everything I had into that car—time, money, love. I had learned how to pull motors in and out of it, how to fine-tune every sound from the speakers until the bass shook your chest. That car wasn't just a car—it was freedom. It was control.

But standing there under the flickering glow of a streetlight, I realized something: I couldn't keep running forever.

The streets were a cycle—a deadly one. And I was caught in it, spinning endlessly, hoping I wouldn't fly off the edge. But deep down, I knew I had to find a way out.

I thought about my best friend again. I thought about all the promises we made to each other, all the dreams we had. I owed it to him to make something of myself—to carry his memory with me in every step I took forward.

But moving forward meant making sacrifices. It meant leaving some people, some habits, and some streets behind.

It wasn't easy. Loyalty kept pulling me back, and survival kept pushing me forward. It was like being caught between two walls closing in on me, and every decision felt like it carried the weight of life or death.

But I knew one thing for certain: I couldn't die with my story untold.

I climbed into the driver's seat of my Caprice, turned the ignition, and let the engine roar to life. The bass thumped through the speakers, and for a moment, it felt like the heartbeat of the city was pulsing through me.

As I pulled away from the curb, I made a silent promise—to myself, to my best friend, and to the streets that raised me:

"I'm gonna make it. For both of us."

32

the funeral that changed everything

The day of his funeral still haunts me.

I woke up that morning with a tightness in my chest, like the weight of the world had collapsed onto my shoulders. The sun was out, bright and bold, like it didn't know the world was darker now, like it didn't care that my best friend wasn't waking up with the rest of us.

I dressed in silence. Black slacks, a black shirt, and shoes polished so clean they could've reflected the face of God Himself. I remember staring at myself in the mirror, seeing a boy trying to wear the face of a man. But grief doesn't care about appearances. It doesn't care how clean your shoes are or how sharp your outfit looks. It just sits heavy in your gut, refusing to let go.

The funeral home smelled like flowers—overwhelming, suffocating, like they were trying to cover up the scent of death itself. People were everywhere, faces I recognized and faces I didn't. Some were crying openly, others held it in like it was a secret they couldn't afford to share. But me? I couldn't cry. I wanted to, but I couldn't. The tears were stuck somewhere deep inside me, frozen behind the wall I had built around my heart.

When I saw him lying in that casket, it felt like someone had taken a baseball bat to my chest. His face was still, peaceful in a way that felt unnatural. He wasn't supposed to be lying there like that. He was supposed to be standing next to me, cracking jokes, talking about the future we both swore we'd reach one day.

But there he was. Still. Silent. Gone.

I stayed back, standing against the wall as people walked by his casket, saying their goodbyes. I couldn't bring myself to step forward. I was afraid—afraid that if I looked too long, if I let myself feel too much, I'd break. And breaking wasn't an option. Not for me. Not in the world I was living in.

But then his mother—his momma—walked up to me. Her eyes were red, her face pale, and her voice was cracked when she spoke.

"He loved you, Imani. You were his brother. Don't ever forget that."

I nodded, but I couldn't speak. What was I supposed to say? *I'm sorry?* Sorry wouldn't bring him back. Sorry wouldn't erase the bullet. Sorry wouldn't stop the ache in her chest or the void in mine.

When they closed the casket, something in me snapped. A piece of me locked itself away, deep inside, where no one could reach it. I realized then that death wasn't just about losing someone—it was about losing a part of yourself with them. And once that part is gone, you don't get it back.

After the funeral, we gathered outside in the parking lot. People hugged, whispered prayers, and shared stories. But the air felt hollow, like the soul of the day had been stripped away. I stood off to the side, hands in my pockets, head down.

That's when Sean walked up to me. His face was hard, unreadable, but his eyes—his eyes carried the same weight I felt in my chest.

"You good?" he asked.

I nodded, but we both knew I was lying.

"We gotta keep movin'," he said. "He'd want that."

I wanted to believe him, but moving forward felt impossible. The streets didn't give time to grieve. There were no pauses, no timeouts, no breaks. You buried your dead, wiped your face, and got back to surviving. That's how it worked. But deep down, I knew I couldn't keep living like this forever. Every day felt like walking a tightrope over an open grave, and one wrong step could send me tumbling into the darkness below.

That night, I found myself alone in my cream Chevy Caprice. The speakers thumped, the bass rattled the frame of the car, but the music couldn't drown out the noise in my head.

I gripped the steering wheel so tight my knuckles turned white. My head was spinning with thoughts, regrets, and anger. Anger at the streets, anger at myself, anger at God for letting this happen.

I slammed my fist against the dashboard, the sound sharp and loud in the confined space of the car.

"Why him?! WHY?!"

The silence that followed felt suffocating. I leaned my head against the steering wheel, my chest heaving, my eyes squeezed shut. And for the first time since it happened, I let the tears fall. Silent, heavy, unstoppable.

In that moment, I made a promise to myself. A promise that I would carry him with me in everything I did. That his name, his memory, and his dreams wouldn't be buried with him. They'd live on through me.

But promises are heavy. They're easy to make in moments of grief, but hard to keep when the world keeps throwing punches at you.

I dried my face, started the car, and drove aimlessly through the city. The neon lights blurred together, the streets were alive with people who had no idea how much weight I was carrying in my chest.

I didn't stop driving until the sun started to rise. The orange glow of dawn painted the sky, and for a brief moment, it felt like the world was holding its breath.

I pulled over, stepped out of the car, and looked up at the sky.

"I'll make it out," I said out loud, my voice steady despite the lump in my throat. *"I'll make it out, and I'll make it count. For him. For me. For everyone we lost."*

And in that moment, I knew—no matter how heavy the weight of loss and loyalty felt, I would carry it. I would carry it until the day I couldn't anymore.

But until then… I was still here.

And I wasn't done yet.

<h1 style="text-align:center">33
survival ain't free</h1>

Survival wasn't just a word—it was a way of life. It was waking up every day and stepping into a world where every decision felt like a roll of the dice. It was knowing that the wrong move could mean prison, injury, or worse, a funeral where your face was painted on T-shirts and your name etched on tombstones.

After my best friend's death, the streets felt different. The corners felt colder. The faces around me were harder to trust. Everyone carried their own agenda, their own survival plan, and I couldn't blame them. But that didn't mean I could let my guard down—not for a second.

The Hustle Never Slept

At 16 years old, I was already deep in the game. Hustling wasn't just about money—it was about respect. It was about holding your own, proving you belonged in spaces where weakness was a death sentence. Whether it was flipping cars, rolling dice, or running quick plays, I stayed in motion. Idle hands didn't just breed poverty—they bred vulnerability.

My cream Chevy Caprice became more than just a car—it was my fortress, my office, and my escape pod. I had it sitting low, the sound system knocking so hard it felt like the pavement vibrated when I rolled by. People noticed me, and in a world where being seen could mean being targeted, I had to stay sharp.

But the money? It came fast, and it went even faster.

There were nights when I walked away from the dice game with stacks so thick they barely fit in my pockets. And there were nights when I walked away with nothing but the taste of regret in my mouth. But I kept playing because the streets taught me one thing: *If you're scared of losing, you'll never win.*

The Accident That Almost Ended Everything

It was late. Too late to be out, too late to be sober, and too late to be making the kinds of decisions I was making. I had just left Denby High School after a heated argument with someone who owed me money. My head was hot, my vision blurry with frustration, but I climbed into my Caprice anyway.

The roads were slick with rain, streetlights reflecting off the puddles like broken mirrors. I wasn't driving—I was flying. The engine roared, the bass thumped, and my foot was heavy on the gas.

I don't remember the exact moment it happened. One second, I was gripping the steering wheel, and the next, I was airborne. The sound of glass shattering, metal twisting, and my body being thrown forward—all of it happened in slow motion.

When I woke up, I was halfway through the windshield, blood pouring down the side of my face, my vision swimming in and out of focus. 14 stitches on the right side of my head. That's what it took to put me back together. But the scars on the outside were nothing compared to the ones on the inside.

As I lay in that hospital bed, staring up at the pale ceiling tiles, all I could think about was how close I had come to becoming another story. Another name whispered in the streets, another funeral someone had to dress up for, another ghost haunting the corners I used to stand on.

But I wasn't gone. Not yet. And if God gave me another shot, then I damn sure wasn't going to waste it.

Back to the Grind

After the accident, I moved different. I still hustled, still played dice, still made moves, but I carried myself with a sharper edge. There was no room for mistakes now. Every dollar I made, every risk I took —it had to mean something.

But hustling wasn't the only thing I was juggling. I was also fighting battles that didn't have a visible enemy. Custody hearings, courtrooms, and judges who looked at me like I was already guilty before I even spoke.

I remember sitting in that courtroom, wearing my cleanest outfit, my shoes polished, my hands folded in my lap. I spoke respectfully, made eye contact, did everything they told me would work. But it didn't matter. They looked at me and saw a statistic, a story they thought they already knew.

"Mr. Grier, your children will remain in foster care."

Those words cut deeper than any bullet ever could. I had worked two jobs, maintained two cars, kept money in two bank accounts. Each of my kids had their own room, their own furniture, their own space. But none of it mattered to them.

That day, I walked out of the courtroom feeling defeated, but I made a silent promise to myself—and to my kids.

"I'm gonna build something so big, so undeniable, that they'll have no choice but to see me. No choice but to respect me."

The Turning Point

The streets had given me a master's degree in survival, but survival wasn't enough anymore. I wanted a **legacy**. I wanted something that couldn't be snatched away by a judge, a rival, or a bad roll of the dice.

That's when music started calling me louder than ever.

I had always loved music—its power to tell stories, to heal, to connect. But now it felt like more than just an escape. It felt like *a mission*. I started spending more time writing; crafting verses that carried my pain, my joy, my struggles, and my dreams.

At first, it was just me and a pen, scribbling in notebooks late at night under the dim glow of a cracked lampshade. But then… it grew. People started listening. They started feeling what I was saying. And that's when I realized: I could reach people. I could change people. I could heal people.

But the hustle? It didn't stop. It couldn't stop. Because dreams didn't pay bills, and music didn't fill empty stomachs—not yet, anyway.

As the chapter of my life started shifting from survival to purpose, I felt something I hadn't felt in a long time: hope.

But hope, just like survival, came at a price. And I was willing to pay it.

The question was—how much more was life going to ask of me before I could finally breathe?

34

the crossroads of destiny

*L*ife has a way of bringing you to a crossroads—moments where one decision can change everything. Some choices are loud and obvious, like standing face-to-face with a man holding a gun. Others are quiet, creeping up on you in the stillness of the night while you're staring at the ceiling, trying to make sense of your life.

I was standing at one of those crossroads, and I could feel it deep in my chest.

The Weight of the Hustle

The streets had given me everything and taken just as much. Money came and went. Friends became enemies. Opportunities turned into regrets. But one thing stayed consistent: the hunger for more.

I wasn't satisfied with just surviving anymore. I wanted *something real*. Something that couldn't be taken away by a bad roll of the dice or a crooked cop with an agenda.

But walking away from the hustle wasn't easy. It was familiar, comfortable even, like an old jacket with bloodstains you learned to ignore.

One night, I found myself sitting in my cream Chevy Caprice, the engine idling, the bass from the speakers rattling the windows. The cash I had made from a dice game earlier that night sat heavy in my lap, bundled in rubber bands.

I counted it—once, twice—my fingers moving with muscle memory.

But as I stared at the stack of money, something in me shifted.

"Is this it?" I whispered to myself. *"Is this what I want my life to look like forever?"*

The answer came to me so clearly it felt like someone had whispered it directly into my ear: No.

I had tasted death, felt the sting of loss, and carried the weight of guilt on my back like a sack of bricks. I had been stitched back together, not just physically, but emotionally, time and time again. And for what? To risk it all every single night?

No. I needed *more*.

But wanting more and getting more were two entirely different things.

The Birth of a Dream

Music had always been there—a quiet hum in the background of my life. Whether it was blasting from car speakers, echoing through dice game alleys, or playing faintly in the corner of someone's house party, it was always *there*.

But now? Now, it was becoming *everything*.

I started spending nights in small studios, trading money I made hustling for hours behind a mic. Every verse I wrote felt like therapy. Every beat drop felt like a breath of fresh air.

My pain, my struggle, my story—I poured it all into those songs.

But it wasn't just about me anymore. I started noticing something: people were listening.

Kids from the same neighborhoods I grew up in would come up to me after hearing one of my songs and say things like, *"Yo, that verse hit me, bro. That's my life too."*

It wasn't about chasing fame or stacking platinum plaques. It was about *connection*. About reaching someone who felt invisible, unheard, forgotten.

But music wasn't paying the bills—*not yet*. And reality doesn't wait for dreams to catch up.

So I kept one foot in the streets and one foot in the studio, trying to balance two worlds that didn't mix.

The Betrayal That Changed Everything

One of the hardest lessons the streets teach you is that not everyone you break bread with wants to see you eat.

There was someone—I'll keep his name out of this for now—but he was close. Someone I trusted. Someone I had looked out for when he was down, fed when he was hungry, and covered when the wolves were circling.

But loyalty is a double-edged sword.

One night, we had set up a deal—money was involved, heavy money. I showed up ready, cautious but confident. But the vibe was off. Have you ever walked into a room and felt like the air's been poisoned? Like the walls are watching you? That's what it felt like.

Long story short, he set me up.

Guns drawn, money snatched, trust shattered. I was left on my knees in an empty building, my own blood pooling on the floor from where the barrel of a pistol had cracked against my temple.

But they didn't pull the trigger.

Why? I'll never know. Maybe it was luck. Maybe it was God. Maybe it was guilt.

All I knew was that I walked out of that building alive, and something inside me snapped.

I realized that night that if I didn't change, I was going to end up in one of two places: dead or in prison.

There was no third option. No fairytale ending waiting for me in the streets.

The Decision

I drove around for hours after that night, blood dried on my face, my body aching, but my mind sharper than it had ever been.

I thought about my kids—Imani, Pepper, and Terrell—their faces flashing in my mind like photos in a slideshow.

I thought about my best friend in his casket, about the funerals I had attended, about the funerals I had narrowly avoided attending as the guest of honor.

And I thought about *music*.

About the way it felt to stand in front of a mic and spill my soul into a beat. About the way a song could make someone feel seen, heard, understood.

I pulled over, parked my car on an empty street, and sat in silence.

"I'm done," I said out loud. *"I'm done with this life. I'm going all in on music. All in on something real."*

It wasn't an easy decision. It wasn't clean or pretty. The streets don't let you go without a fight, and I knew there would be consequences.

But I was ready.

Because for the first time in a long time, I wasn't just surviving anymore—I was chasing something.

A dream. A legacy. A future.

And no matter what came next, I wasn't turning back.

35
all in or nothing

When you decide to leave the streets behind, the streets don't just wave goodbye and wish you luck. They cling to you, pull at you, whisper in your ear like a jealous lover who can't accept you've moved on. Walking away wasn't as simple as just saying, *"I'm done."*

It was war.

War with myself. War with my habits. War with the people who saw me as nothing more than a source of money, power, or leverage. But I had made a promise—to myself, to my kids, to my best friend who never got the chance to leave.

Burning Bridges

The first step was cutting ties—ties that had been years in the making. Friendships, partnerships, deals—all of it had to go. And it wasn't clean. You can't tell people who are drowning in the same ocean as you that you're suddenly climbing onto a lifeboat. They don't want to hear it.

"You think you better than us now?"

"You really think you gonna make it out there in the music game?"

"Bro, the streets made you. You ain't nothin' without this."

Those words cut deep because part of me wondered if they were right. Who was I without the streets? Without the dice games, the quick money, the late-night moves? Could I really make it out there in the world of music, in studios filled with people who didn't know my story, who didn't know my hunger?

But every time doubt crept in, I reminded myself: *You already beat death. You already survived the worst. There's nothing scarier than what you've already been through.*

One by one, I started walking away from people who couldn't see the vision. People who would've rather dragged me back down than let me climb out. And it hurt. But I knew it had to be done.

Building from the Ground Up

Music wasn't a guaranteed paycheck. It wasn't a stable nine-to-five with benefits and vacation days. It was a risk. But it was my risk—one I was willing to take.

I started investing everything I had into my music. Every extra dollar went into studio time, equipment, beats, and marketing. I studied the game—not just the art, but the *business*. I watched interviews, read books, analyzed contracts. I wasn't going to let someone else exploit me just because I was hungry to make it.

Late nights turned into early mornings. I'd spend hours writing, rewriting, recording, and then listening back to every word. Every bar had to mean something. Every verse had to carry weight.

But beyond the music, I started thinking bigger.

"What if I could use music to help others?"

"What if I could change someone's life the way music changed mine?"

That's when the seeds of World of Music started planting themselves in my mind. I didn't just want to make songs—I wanted to make a *difference*.

I wanted to go into schools, into community centers, into spaces where kids felt lost and forgotten, and show them: "Your voice matters. Your story matters. Your dreams matter."

But dreams don't build themselves. They need sweat, sacrifice, and time.

The Sacrifice

When you're chasing a dream, you start to realize how much you have to sacrifice. Time with family. Sleep. Stability. There were weeks where my fridge was empty, where the gas tank was running on fumes, where every bill collector seemed to have my number on speed dial.

But I kept going.

I started performing at local events, showing up to open mics, handing out flyers for my shows. I wasn't too proud to hustle for my music the same way I had hustled in the streets. But the difference was, this hustle felt *clean*. It felt *right*.

And people started noticing.

At one show, after performing a song that I had poured my soul into, a young kid came up to me afterward. He couldn't have been older than 13. He tugged on my sleeve and said, *"Yo, that song… it felt like you were talkin' to me. I needed to hear that."*

Man… that moment hit different. It wasn't about the applause, the likes, or the followers. It was about *connection*. About reaching someone who needed to hear what I had to say.

The Temptation to Go Back

But the streets… they don't let go easy. Every time money got tight, every time a bill came due, every time someone hit my line with an "opportunity" to make some fast cash, the temptation was there.

It would've been so easy to slide back. To roll one more set of dice. To flip one more car. To take one more risk.

But every time I thought about going back, I thought about my kids. I thought about their faces, their laughter, the moments I was fighting to create for them. And I thought about my best friend, lying in that casket, his dreams buried with him.

Going back wasn't an option. Not anymore.

The Turning Point

One night, after performing at a community event, someone approached me. A woman with a kind smile and a clipboard in her hand. She said she was with a local school district, and she had been watching me perform.

"Have you ever thought about working with kids? About using your music to teach them something?"

That question was like a spark hitting gasoline.

I nodded. "Yeah. Yeah, I've thought about it."

That was the beginning of something bigger than me. Something I couldn't have imagined back when I was just a kid throwing dice behind liquor stores.

It was the start of World of Music—not just an idea anymore, but a *reality*.

All In

This wasn't just about survival anymore. This was about *legacy*. About breaking cycles, opening doors, and showing kids from neighborhoods like mine that they could dream bigger than the block they grew up on.

But this road wasn't smooth. There were still obstacles ahead, still people waiting to see me fail, still nights where doubt crept in like an old friend.

But I was ready.

Because when you've already stared death in the face, failure doesn't seem so scary anymore.

And as I lay in bed that night, staring at the ceiling, I whispered to myself:

"All in or nothing. Let's get it."

36
building the blueprint

When you decide to build something from the ground up, it's not just about having a dream—it's about having a plan. Dreams are pretty. Plans are gritty. Dreams make people smile. Plans make people sweat. And in those early days of turning World of Music into reality, I learned quickly that dreams without action are just wishes floating in the wind.

The First Brick

The day after that conversation with the woman from the school district, I sat down with an old, beat-up notebook and a pen. I wrote at the top of the first page: "World of Music: Changing Lives Through Sound."

It wasn't just a catchy tagline. It was my mission.

I started writing down everything I wanted this program to represent:

- Healing: Helping kids find a way to express their pain and struggles through music.
- Empowerment: Teaching them how to write songs, perform, and use their voices to be heard.
- Growth: Showing them that music isn't just an art—it's a tool. A tool for survival, a tool for expression, a tool for change.

But writing it down was one thing. Bringing it to life was something else entirely.

I needed funding. I needed support. I needed spaces to host workshops. And I didn't have any of those things. But I had determination, and sometimes, that's the most valuable resource of all.

The Hustle Reimagined

I started hitting up schools, community centers, and local youth programs. Anywhere there were kids, I was there. I didn't have polished brochures or corporate-level presentations—I had my voice, my story, and my vision.

"Listen, I know these kids. I've been these kids. And I know what music can do for them because it saved me. Let me show them how to use their voice. Let me show them how to heal."

Some people looked at me sideways. Some people nodded politely and said they'd "get back to me." But every now and then, someone would lean forward, eyes locked on mine, and say, *"Okay. Show us what you can do."*

And every time I got that chance, I gave it everything I had.

The First Workshop

I'll never forget the first official World of Music workshop. It was in a small classroom in a community center. The desks were scratched, the whiteboard was stained, and the fluorescent lights buzzed faintly overhead.

There were about ten kids sitting in that room, all of them slouched in their chairs, faces blank, like they had already decided this was going to be just another boring "after-school program."

I walked in, set my backpack down, and pulled out a speaker and a mic.

"Alright, y'all," I said, my voice calm but firm. "I'm not here to waste your time, and I don't want you to waste mine. I'm here because I know what it feels like to hurt. I know what it feels like to be angry. I know what it feels like to want to scream but not know if anyone's listening. But today? Today, we're gonna let it out. Through music. Through words. Through this mic right here."

The room got quiet. Some of them sat up straighter. A couple of them nodded.

We started small—freewriting exercises, simple rhyme schemes, basic hooks. And then something happened. One of the kids—a quiet girl sitting in the back with her hood pulled low over her eyes—stood up and walked to the mic.

Her voice was shaky at first, her words uncertain, but as she started to rap the verse she had written, something changed. Her voice grew stronger, her posture straightened, and by the time she finished, there were tears in her eyes.

The room erupted in applause. And in that moment, I realized: This is it. This is the work. This is the mission.

The Momentum

Word started to spread. The kids talked. The staff at the community center talked. Before long, I was getting calls from other schools, other centers, other people who had heard about *"that guy who's teaching kids to rap their pain out."*

But momentum doesn't mean stability. I was still juggling side hustles, side gigs, and side prayers to keep the lights on and gas in my tank. There were nights I went to sleep hungry, nights where I sat in my car staring at the ceiling, wondering if this was all worth it.

But every time I doubted, I'd get a text or a call from one of the kids.

"Yo, Mr. Grier, I wrote another verse. Can I send it to you?"

"Thank you for listening to me, bro. Nobody ever listens."

Those moments kept me going.

The Pushback

But not everyone was rooting for me.

Some people from my past started creeping back into the picture. Old faces, old habits, old temptations.

"You still out here chasin' that dream, huh? Man, come back to the block. We got money over here."

"Bro, that music stuff ain't paying your bills. You know what will."

It was like having the devil whispering in one ear and my dream whispering in the other. And every day, I had to make a choice about which voice to listen to.

But here's the thing about purpose—it's louder than doubt if you let it be.

The Breakthrough

The day I got a call from a local news station asking me to come on air and talk about *World of Music* felt unreal. I remember sitting in the green room, mic clipped to my collar, my heart pounding in my chest.

When the camera lights turned on and the host asked me about my program, about why I do what I do, I said one thing:

"Because every kid deserves to be heard. Every kid deserves to feel like their story matters. And if I can give them a mic, if I can give them a beat, and if I can give them a stage to stand on, then I've done my job."

When that interview aired, everything changed. Schools started reaching out. Grants started coming in. And for the first time, it felt like I wasn't just fighting to survive—I was building something *real*.

What's Next?

But success isn't a final chapter—it's just a new beginning. I wasn't done. I wasn't even close.

World of Music wasn't just a workshop anymore—it was becoming a **movement**.

And as I stood onstage at one of our first big events, watching the kids perform songs they had written themselves, tears streaming down their faces as they poured their hearts into the mic, I realized:

This wasn't just about me anymore.

It was about *them*. Their voices. Their stories. Their futures.

And I was just getting started.

37
from vision to reality

Turning a dream into reality isn't a straight path—it's a winding road filled with potholes, detours, and roadblocks. And *World of Music* was no different. For every "yes" I got, there were five "no's." For every breakthrough, there was a setback waiting in the shadows. But the thing about me? I don't quit. I've been knocked down, left for dead, and counted out more times than I can remember, but every time, I got back up.

Because this wasn't just about me anymore—it was about the kids.

The First Big Event

When the first *World of Music showcase* came together, it felt like magic. It wasn't just a workshop in a dusty classroom anymore—it was a stage, lights, a mic, and an audience.

The kids were nervous. I could see it in their eyes—the way their hands shook as they clutched their lyric sheets, the way they kept glancing at the crowd as it started to fill up.

"Listen," I told them backstage. "Every person in that audience is here because they want to hear *you*. Your story. Your voice. Don't hold back. Don't second-guess yourself. Go out there and own that stage."

The first kid stepped up to the mic—a young boy, barely 14, with a voice so shaky I thought he might crumble right there. But then the beat dropped, and something shifted. His words came out sharp, his confidence grew with every bar, and by the time he finished, the crowd was on their feet, clapping, whistling, and shouting his name.

One by one, the kids performed. And one by one, they proved to themselves—and everyone in that room—that their voices mattered.

By the end of the night, the kids were glowing. Smiling. Hugging each other. You could feel it in the air: something special had happened.

But the moment that stuck with me the most was when one of the quietest kids—the same girl from the first workshop—walked up to me after her performance, tears streaming down her face.

"Thank you, Mr. Grier. Nobody ever told me I was good at anything before."

Man… if that doesn't hit you in your chest, nothing will.

Growing Pains

Success brings growth, and growth brings growing pains.

More schools wanted the program. More kids were showing up. More people were reaching out. And with growth came pressure.

I was still juggling side hustles, trying to keep food on the table and gas in the tank while running workshops, coordinating events, and managing a growing team of volunteers. I had no business degree, no rich investors backing me—just hustle, heart, and a vision I refused to let go of.

There were days when the weight of it all felt like too much. Days when I wondered if I was crazy for thinking I could pull this off. Days when I stared at a stack of unpaid bills and thought about all the people who told me this wouldn't work.

But every time doubt crept in, I remembered those kids. I remembered the way their faces lit up after performing, the way they poured their hearts into their lyrics, the way they hugged me after every workshop.

I couldn't let them down.

The Battle Behind the Scenes

But with growth comes challenges.

The money wasn't coming in fast enough to match the demand.

Equipment was breaking down. Spaces were hard to book. And while the world was starting to pay attention, the bills didn't stop piling up.

I remember one night sitting in my car, staring at a spreadsheet on my laptop, trying to figure out how I was going to make it all work. The numbers didn't add up. The funding wasn't there. And the weight of it all sat heavy on my shoulders.

But quitting? Nah. That wasn't an option.

I started reaching out to anyone and everyone. Local businesses. Community leaders. Grant programs. I wrote proposals, sent emails, made phone calls until my voice was hoarse. Some people slammed doors in my face. Others didn't respond at all.

But a few… a few said yes. And sometimes, a few is all you need.

The Kids Who Changed Me

The more time I spent in these workshops, the more I realized something: these kids weren't just students—they were teachers. They taught me about resilience, about creativity, about the raw, unfiltered honesty that comes out when you hand someone a mic and tell them, *"Say whatever's on your heart."*

There was one kid—I'll call him Marcus.

Marcus came to the workshop with anger in his eyes and pain in his voice. He barely spoke to anyone, sat in the back, and avoided eye contact. But one day, I handed him a pen and told him, *"Write it down. Whatever it is. Don't hold back."*

The verse he wrote… man, it stopped the whole room. He rapped about losing his mom, about feeling abandoned, about wanting to give up but holding on because of his little sister.

By the end of it, he was crying. And so was everyone else in that room, including me.

Music wasn't just saving these kids—it was saving me, too.

The Bigger Picture

World of Music wasn't just growing—it was evolving. It wasn't just about workshops anymore. It was about creating opportunities, building confidence, and showing these kids that their stories *mattered*.

But this was only the beginning.

Because deep down, I knew: We were just getting started.

And I wasn't stopping until *World of Music* became bigger than me

—bigger than all of us. A legacy that would outlive me, my scars, and the streets that tried to bury me.

I leaned back in my chair one night, staring at a blank piece of paper, and wrote one sentence at the top:

"Dream bigger, Imani. Dream bigger."

38

when purpose outgrew the pain

There comes a moment in every journey when you realize you're no longer walking just for yourself. Your feet are moving, your heart is beating, and your soul is burning with a purpose so big it feels like it might consume you. For me, that moment wasn't loud. It wasn't flashy. It didn't come with cameras or applause.

It happened on an ordinary day, in an ordinary workshop, with an extraordinary kid.

The Boy with No Voice

It was a Wednesday afternoon. The fluorescent lights in the school gym buzzed faintly, and the smell of sweat and cleaning chemicals hung in the air. The kids shuffled in, dragging their feet, eyes glued to their phones. Some sat in the back, arms crossed, faces blank.

But one boy stood out. He wasn't the loudest. In fact, he wasn't saying anything at all. He sat near the exit door, his head down, hood pulled low, his backpack still on his shoulders like he wasn't planning to stay long. His name was Andre.

I had seen that look before—the look of someone carrying more weight than their shoulders were built for. The kind of weight that pulls your chin down to your chest and makes every step feel like you're dragging chains behind you.

I walked over and sat on the floor next to him, leaning my back against the wall.

"You good, man?" I asked casually.

He shrugged, still not making eye contact.

"You don't have to be here if you don't want to. But if you do stay, I just need you to know one thing—this is a space where you're safe. Nobody's judging you here. Nobody's laughing at you. We're just talking, vibing, and letting some stuff out."

He didn't respond, but he didn't leave either. That was enough for me.

The Moment the Mic Changed Everything

The workshop began. Kids started writing, scribbling verses in notebooks, tapping their pens against the tables as beats played softly in the background. A few brave ones stepped up to the mic, spitting bars about school, family, dreams, and heartbreak.

But Andre sat still, his notebook blank, his eyes staring into nothing.

At the end of the session, I grabbed the mic and said, "Andre, man, you good? You wanna try it out? You ain't gotta rap if you don't want to. You can just say something. Anything."

For a long moment, he didn't move. Then, slowly, he stood up. His steps were cautious, hesitant, like he was walking across thin ice. He took the mic, held it close to his mouth, and let out a shaky breath.

The gym was dead silent.

"I... I miss my mom," he said softly. "I miss her so much, and I don't know how to stop feeling like it's my fault she's gone."

His voice broke on the last word, and the mic picked up the sound of him holding back tears.

No beat. No bars. Just raw truth. And it hit the room like a grenade.

I walked up, put my hand on his shoulder, and whispered, "It's not your fault, Dre. It's not your fault."

He looked up at me, his face streaked with tears, and for the first time since he walked into that gym, he looked *alive*. Vulnerable, but alive.

The kids started clapping—not the loud, rowdy kind of applause you hear after someone kills a verse, but the soft, understanding kind. The kind of clap that says, *"We hear you. We see you. You're not alone."*

Andre sat back down, his head in his hands, but something had shifted in the air. The weight he carried wasn't gone, but he wasn't carrying it alone anymore.

Purpose Outgrew the Pain

That night, I sat in my car, staring at the raindrops sliding down the windshield. I couldn't stop thinking about Andre. About his voice, his pain, and the way the mic had become a lifeline for him.

I realized something at that moment: World of Music wasn't just a program anymore—it was a bridge.

A bridge for kids like Andre to cross over from isolation to connection, from silence to expression, from hopelessness to possibility.

But it was more than that—it was a lifeline for *me*, too. Every workshop, every verse, every tear-filled confession reminded me why I had chosen this path. The streets taught me survival, but these kids were teaching me *purpose*.

I wasn't just building a program. I was building a safe haven.

The Challenges Kept Coming

But purpose doesn't pay bills. Purpose doesn't fix broken equipment. Purpose doesn't stop school districts from cutting budgets and pulling support.

Every step forward came with new challenges:

• A school pulled out last minute due to funding cuts.

• A promised grant never arrived.

• A broken mic set me back a hundred bucks I didn't have to spare.

There were nights I wanted to quit. Nights where I sat in my car with my head in my hands, asking myself, *"What am I doing? Is this even working?"*

But every time I thought about walking away, I thought about Andre. About the quiet kids in the back of the room. About the verses written in shaky handwriting and delivered with trembling voices.

I thought about how the streets tried to bury me, but God had other plans.

The Unexpected Gift

A month after that workshop, I got a letter. It was from Andre.

"Mr. Grier, thank you for letting me talk. Thank you for telling me it wasn't my fault. I've been writing more. It helps. You helped. I hope one day I can help people like you do."

I folded the letter carefully and slid it into my glovebox.

In a world that tried to tell me I wasn't enough, that I wasn't worthy, that I'd never build something real—I had proof in my hands that I was making a difference.

And if I had to sacrifice sleep, comfort, and even stability to keep doing this, then so be it.

Because for every Andre, there were dozens more kids out there waiting. Waiting for someone to hand them a mic and say, *"Your voice matters."*

Eyes on the Horizon

As the rain tapped softly on the windshield, I whispered to myself, *"Keep going. Keep building. Keep believing."*

Because now I knew:

- *World of Music* wasn't just a program.
- It wasn't just a vision.
- It wasn't just a dream.

It was a calling.

And I wasn't stopping—not now, not ever.

39
the fire within

There's a fire that burns in people who've walked through hell and come out the other side. It's not the kind of fire that fades when things get hard—it's the kind that grows brighter, hotter, more relentless. By this point in my journey, that fire wasn't just in my chest—it was in every step I took, every word I spoke, and every workshop I ran.

But fire, like purpose, needs fuel. And sometimes, that fuel comes from places you don't expect.

The Walls Closing In

The days turned into weeks, the weeks into months. *World of Music* was growing—faster than I could keep up with. Schools were reaching out, emails were piling up, and the phone never stopped buzzing. But behind the scenes, the reality was less glamorous.

The money still wasn't consistent. Some schools wanted the program but couldn't afford to pay. Some promised funding that never arrived. Equipment kept breaking, and I was still juggling side hustles just to keep the lights on.

There were days I sat in my car outside a school, head resting on the steering wheel, praying for strength.

"God, if you want me to keep going, show me something. Give me a sign. Because right now, I don't know if I can do this anymore."

And every time, something—*someone*—would show up to remind me why I couldn't stop.

The Student Who Changed Me

His name was Jamal. Fourteen years old, tall for his age, with a scowl carved permanently onto his face. He came into my workshop one afternoon with his arms crossed, his hood pulled low, and an energy that screamed, *"Don't talk to me."*

He didn't pick up a pen. Didn't even look at the mic. Just sat there, staring at the wall, daring anyone to say something to him.

After the session ended, while the other kids filed out, I stayed behind and sat next to him.

"You wanna tell me what's going on, Jamal?"

Silence.

I waited.

"You don't gotta say anything if you don't want to," I continued. "But I see you, man. I see that weight you're carrying. And I know it's heavy. But you don't have to carry it alone."

His jaw clenched, and for a split second, I thought he was going to get up and walk away. But instead, his shoulders slumped, and he whispered, "I'm just... tired."

I didn't push him to explain. I just nodded.

"Come back next week," I said. "You don't gotta talk. You don't gotta write. Just show up. That's all."

He nodded and walked out the door.

The Breakthrough

Jamal came back the next week. And the week after that. And the week after that.

Slowly, he started writing. His first verses were rough, disjointed, scattered. But they were *honest*. And honesty has a way of cutting through all the noise.

One day, after weeks of building trust, he stood up and walked to the mic. His voice was low at first, like he was afraid of being heard. But as he kept going, his voice grew stronger. His words painted pictures—of nights spent hiding in his room while his parents fought, of losing his older brother to gun violence, of feeling invisible in a world that never stopped to ask if he was okay.

By the time he finished, the room was silent. No clapping, no cheering—just silence. The kind of silence that feels heavy because everyone in the room felt those words in their chest.

When he put the mic down, Jamal looked at me and said, "That felt… good."

"Because it's real," I said. "Your words matter, Jamal. Don't ever forget that."

Fighting for the Dream

Moments like that kept me going, but they didn't pay the bills.

I started applying for grants, pitching to community leaders, and meeting with school district boards. Every meeting felt like a battle. I'd walk into these polished conference rooms, wearing my best outfit, carrying binders full of data, testimonials, and proposals.

But no matter how much passion I spoke with, there were always people who just didn't *get it*.

"Mr. Grier, this program is admirable, but it's not sustainable."

"How do we know these kids are really benefiting?"

"What happens when the funding runs out?"

I wanted to grab them by the collar and scream, *"Come to a workshop! Look these kids in the eye! Listen to their stories! Tell me they're not benefiting!"*

But instead, I smiled, I answered their questions, and I walked out with my head high, even when the answer was "no."

Because every "no" brought me closer to a "yes." And I only needed one.

The Breakthrough Grant

One day, I got an email.

"Congratulations! Your program has been selected for funding under the Youth Empowerment Initiative."

I had to read it three times to make sure I wasn't seeing things. It wasn't life-changing money, but it was enough to breathe—to replace broken equipment, to secure spaces for workshops, to give me a little room to stop hustling side jobs just to keep things afloat.

When the check arrived, I sat in my car staring at it, tears blurring my vision.

"We made it," I whispered. *"We're still here."*

But I knew this wasn't the end. It was just a milestone—one step on a long, uphill climb.

A Promise to Myself

That night, as I sat in my car, the city lights reflecting off the windshield, I made a promise:

"No matter how hard it gets, no matter how heavy it feels, I will not stop. Because these kids deserve someone who refuses to give up on them."

The fire inside me was burning hotter than ever, and I wasn't afraid of the flames. I had walked through fire before, and I came out stronger every single time.

This wasn't just my dream anymore—it was our dream.

And I was willing to fight for it until my last breath.

40
the weight of the mission

When people talk about success, they often talk about the glow-up—the highlight reels, the standing ovations, the magazine covers, and the applause. But nobody talks about the *weight* that comes with it. The nights you can't sleep because your mind won't stop racing, the mornings you wake up already exhausted, and the crushing responsibility of knowing that if you fail, it's not just you who loses—it's everyone who's counting on you.

World of Music had become bigger than me. It was no longer just an idea in my notebook or a dream I whispered to myself at night. It was real, and it was growing fast. But with growth came pressure, and with pressure came moments that tested every piece of me.

The Breaking Point

There was a week that I'll never forget.

Three workshops scheduled. Two schools pulled out at the last minute because of funding cuts. My car broke down on the way to the third workshop, leaving me stranded on the side of the road with a trunk full of sound equipment and a heart full of frustration.

I sat on the curb, head in my hands, as cars sped past me on the freeway.

"Why does it always feel like one step forward, two steps back?"

I could feel myself unraveling—mentally, emotionally, spiritually. It felt like the weight of the world was pressing down on my chest, and no matter how hard I pushed back, it wasn't budging.

That night, after getting my car towed and dragging my equipment back home, I sat in the dark in my living room, staring at the floor.

I thought about quitting.

I thought about walking away from it all—World of Music, the workshops, the kids—everything.

But then I thought about Andre. I thought about Jamal. I thought about every quiet kid who stepped up to the mic and found their voice. And I realized that this wasn't just about me. It never was.

I grabbed a piece of paper, scribbled one sentence on it, and taped it to my wall:

"You can't save everyone, but you can change someone."

That night, I made a promise to myself: *No matter how heavy it gets, no matter how much it hurts, I will not quit.*

The Night Everything Changed

A few weeks later, we held a showcase at a local school. It wasn't fancy—just a small stage in a dusty gymnasium, folding chairs lined up in rows, and a handful of parents scattered in the audience. But to me? It felt like Madison Square Garden.

The kids had been preparing for weeks. They wrote their verses, practiced their delivery, and poured their hearts into every word.

When the show started, the first kid stepped onto the stage. A small girl, no older than twelve, clutching the mic so tight her knuckles turned white.

Her voice trembled at first, but as she went on, her words cut through the silence like a knife:

"I wake up in the dark, mama's gone, daddy's gone / All I got is this pen, tryna right every wrong / They told me I'm nothing, they told me I'd fail / But look at me now, I'm tellin' my tale."

The crowd erupted in applause, but I was frozen in place.

That verse—it was her life. Her pain. Her truth. And she had just handed it to us, raw and unfiltered.

As more kids performed, I realized something: This wasn't just music. This was survival. This was healing. This was power.

Facing the Critics

But not everyone saw it that way.

After the event, a school administrator pulled me aside.

"This was great, Mr. Grier, but some of the topics these kids are rapping about… they're heavy. Maybe we can lighten things up next time?"

I stared at him for a long moment before I replied.

"Sir, these kids don't have the privilege of 'lightening things up.' They're living this. Every day. And if they can't say it here, where can they say it?"

He didn't have an answer. And honestly, I didn't expect one.

But it made me realize something: The world isn't always ready for the truth these kids are carrying. But that doesn't mean they should stop speaking it.

The Invitation That Shifted Everything

One day, I got an email that made my heart stop.

"We'd like to invite you to speak at the annual Youth Empowerment Conference."

It was a statewide event—a chance to speak to educators, policymakers, and community leaders about *World of Music*.

I felt the pressure instantly. This wasn't a classroom. This wasn't a gymnasium. This was a *stage* in front of hundreds of people who could either open doors or slam them shut.

On the day of the conference, I stood backstage, my hands trembling, my stomach doing flips. I closed my eyes, took a deep breath, and whispered to myself:

"This isn't about you. This is about them."

When I walked onto that stage, the spotlight felt blinding. But as I began to speak, everything else faded away.

I told them about Andre. About Jamal. About the little girl who stood on stage and poured her soul into her verse. I told them about the weight these kids carried and the way music gave them a way to put it down, even if just for a moment.

By the time I finished, the crowd was silent. Then, one by one, people started standing. The applause was deafening.

And in that moment, I knew: The world was starting to listen.

The Bigger Fight

But that conference wasn't the finish line—it was just another checkpoint.

Because while applause feels good, it doesn't keep the lights on. It doesn't pay for new equipment. It doesn't expand programs to reach more kids.

I realized I needed a team. I needed people who believed in this vision as much as I did. People who could help me build something that would last long after I was gone.

I started reaching out—friends, mentors, volunteers. And slowly, a team began to form. People who showed up, who believed, who sacrificed.

But the fight wasn't over. There were still doubters. Still roadblocks. Still moments that tested me in ways I couldn't have imagined.

A Fire That Won't Go Out

One night, after another long day of meetings, workshops, and endless emails, I sat alone in my car, staring at the city lights in the distance.

I thought about everything it had taken to get here—the scars, the sacrifices, the losses. But I also thought about the kids, about their stories, about their victories.

And I realized something: The fire inside me wasn't going out anytime soon.

"We're not done yet," I whispered to myself. *"Not even close."*

The weight was heavy, but I had learned how to carry it. And as long as there was breath in my lungs and beats in my heart, I was going to keep pushing, keep building, and keep believing.

Because this wasn't just my story anymore—it was our story.

And we were just getting started.

41

bridges and burdens

t this point in my life, the weight of *World of Music* was more than just a responsibility—it was a bridge. A bridge between my past and my future, between pain and healing, between the streets I came from and the stages I was now standing on. But being the bridge comes with its own burden. You're not just holding up your dreams—you're holding up everyone who's depending on you to cross.

And I was starting to feel it in my bones.

The Cost of Carrying Everyone

The emails kept coming. The phone never stopped ringing. Schools wanted more workshops, more kids wanted spaces in the program, and more people wanted me to show up, speak, inspire, perform. On the outside, it looked like everything was falling into place.

But on the inside? I was exhausted.

It's one thing to grind when you're fighting for yourself—it's something entirely different when you're fighting for hundreds of kids who see you as their light in the dark. Every time I thought about slowing down, I pictured their faces. I thought about Andre, Jamal, the little girl on stage pouring her soul into a mic.

"They're counting on you, Imani."

But my body wasn't keeping up with my mind. I wasn't sleeping. I wasn't eating right. And every now and then, I'd catch myself zoning out in the middle of a workshop, my mind somewhere else, drifting into a fog of exhaustion and anxiety.

I had given everything I had to build this bridge. But if I wasn't careful, I was going to collapse under the weight of it.

A Lesson in Letting Go

It was a conversation with an old friend that shook me out of my spiral.

We were sitting in my car, parked in an empty lot after midnight. The engine was off, the only light coming from a flickering streetlamp a few feet away.

"You can't save everybody, bro," he said. "You're running yourself into the ground, trying to carry all this weight by yourself."

"But if I stop, if I slow down, it'll all fall apart," I said, my voice cracking.

He shook his head. "That's the thing—you built something real, man. You built something strong. But you gotta trust other people to help carry it. You gotta let go of the idea that you're the only one who can hold it all together."

That conversation hit me hard. Because he was right. *World of Music* wasn't just about me anymore—it was about the team I had started building, the volunteers who showed up every week, the kids who were stepping up to lead workshops of their own.

I couldn't do everything. And I wasn't supposed to.

Fatherhood in the Shadows

In the middle of all of this, there was another weight I carried every single day: the absence of my kids.

Every morning when I woke up, their faces were the first thing on my mind. Every night before I closed my eyes, I whispered their names like a prayer: Imani, Pepper, Terrell.

The system had told me "no" too many times. The courts had slammed doors in my face, told me I wasn't fit, told me that distance was more important than love, that paperwork was more valuable than presence.

But they couldn't take away the memories.

- Cutting their umbilical cords.
- Doing my daughter's hair before school.
- Taking them to the park, watching their eyes light up at every new adventure.

I kept a picture of them on my desk. Every time I felt like quitting, I'd look at it and remind myself: *Everything I'm building is for them. Every sacrifice, every sleepless night, every broken piece of me—I'm rebuilding it into something they can stand on one day.*

But the silence hurt. The unanswered calls, the letters that never came, the birthdays spent wondering if they missed me too. It was a hole in my chest that nothing—not money, not success, not applause— could ever fill.

When Dreams Start Talking Back

One night, I was driving home from an event. The kids had performed beautifully, the crowd had clapped, and everyone was smiling. But as I sat alone in my car, the weight crept back in.

The radio was low, playing some old-school R&B track, and the city lights blurred as I sped down the empty streets.

I started talking out loud, like someone was sitting in the passenger seat.

"God, if this is where I'm supposed to be, show me. If I'm on the right path, let me know, because I'm tired, man. I'm tired."

The silence that followed felt heavy. But then... something happened.

A text popped up on my phone from a number I didn't recognize.

"Hey, Mr. Grier, it's Andre. I just wanted to say thank you. For everything. I wrote a song tonight, and it made me feel better. You saved me, man. For real."

I pulled over and sat there for a long time, staring at that text, tears pooling in my eyes.

God doesn't always answer loud. Sometimes He whispers. And that night, He whispered through a fourteen-year-old boy named Andre.

A Step Back to Move Forward

I realized something important that night: If I was going to keep carrying this mission, I had to take care of myself too.

I started making small changes:

•Taking time for myself, even if it was just an hour in the morning to sit in silence and breathe.

•Asking for help when I needed it—letting my team step up and take on more responsibility.

•Reminding myself that *it's okay to pause. It's okay to rest. It's okay to be human.*

And something amazing started happening: *World of Music* kept growing. Even when I wasn't burning myself out. Even when I wasn't running on fumes.

It grew because it was no longer about me—it was about us. About the kids, the team, the community.

Looking at the Horizon

One afternoon, I stood in the back of a school auditorium, watching a group of kids rehearse for an upcoming *World of Music* showcase. They were laughing, sharing verses, hyping each other up.

I leaned against the wall and smiled.

This wasn't a workshop anymore—it was a family. And families grow. Families evolve. Families support each other.

I thought about my kids again—Imani, Pepper, and Terrell. I imagined them standing on that stage one day, looking out into the crowd, knowing that their father had built something beautiful.

But I wasn't done yet. Not even close.

I closed my eyes, took a deep breath, and whispered:

"Thank you, God. For the pain. For the purpose. For the fire. I'm ready for whatever comes next."

42

the night everything almost ended

There are moments in life that become etched into your soul. Moments where time slows down, and every detail—every sound, every smell, every flicker of light—burns itself into your memory. For me, one of those moments happened on a night when everything almost ended.

This isn't just a story—it's *a warning*. A reminder that life can change in an instant, and sometimes, survival isn't about strength—it's about grace.

The Setup

It was one of those nights where the air felt heavy, like the city itself was holding its breath. I was 16 years old, young, reckless, and convinced I was untouchable. My cream Chevy Caprice sat low on its tires, the sound system in the back thumping loud enough to rattle nearby windows.

I had just left a dice game, a fat stack of cash stuffed into my pocket, adrenaline still buzzing in my veins from the last roll. The streets were quiet, but something about the night felt *off*.

But I ignored it. I had money in my pocket, music in my ears, and the arrogance of youth shielding me from the reality of how fast everything can change.

I pulled up to a liquor store on Gratiot, just down the block from my uncle Mike's car wash, *Time to Shine*. It was a routine stop—grab a drink, maybe chat with someone outside, and keep it moving. But that night, fate had other plans.

The Gunshot

I didn't wait. My feet moved before my mind could process what was happening. I turned and bolted back toward my car, my sneakers slapping against the cracked pavement.

Pop!

The sound of a gunshot cracked through the night.

I felt it before I heard it—the sharp sting in my side, the burning heat spreading through my skin. But I didn't stop. Adrenaline is a hell of a thing. My brain refused to let my body acknowledge the pain.

I dove into my Caprice, slammed the door, and turned the key so fast I nearly broke it off in the ignition. The engine roared to life, and I punched the gas pedal with everything I had.

The tires screeched. Smoke rose from the pavement. I didn't look back.

The Drive

Blood was soaking through my shirt, warm and sticky against my skin. My side was on fire, every bump in the road sending jolts of pain through my body. But I kept driving.

I don't remember how long I drove or how far I went. Everything outside the car blurred together—streetlights, shadows, distant sirens. My vision started to tunnel, the edges growing dark.

I kept hearing my mother's voice in my head.

"Don't let the streets take you, Imani. You hear me? Don't let them take you."

I don't know if it was luck, instinct, or some kind of divine intervention, but I ended up pulling into a hospital parking lot. I stumbled out of the car, clutching my side, leaving bloody handprints on the hood of my Caprice.

The last thing I remember was collapsing in the ER lobby, the bright fluorescent lights glaring down at me.

The Aftermath

When I woke up, the first thing I felt was the cold, sterile air of the hospital room. My side was wrapped tight, and every breath felt like I was inhaling glass. Machines beeped softly around me, and for a moment, I didn't know where I was.

Then it hit me—the liquor store, the gunshot, the drive.

I was still alive.

A nurse walked in and gave me a sad smile. "You're lucky, you know. A few inches to the left, and we wouldn't be having this conversation."

Lucky. That word echoed in my head. Was it luck, though? Or was it something else?

I stared at the ceiling for hours that night, replaying everything in my head—the faces of those men, the sound of the gunshot, the weight of survival pressing against my chest.

A Visit That Broke Me

A few days later, my mom walked into the hospital room.

Her face was etched with worry and exhaustion; her lips pressed into a thin line as she sat down in the chair next to my bed.

"What did I tell you, Terrell?" she said softly, her voice trembling. "I told you these streets don't love you. I told you they'd take you if you let them."

I couldn't look at her. The weight of her words felt heavier than the bullet wound in my side.

"I'm sorry, Ma," I whispered, my throat tight.

"No, son. Don't apologize to me. Apologize to yourself. Because you deserve better than this. You deserve *more* than this."

She reached out and grabbed my hand, squeezing it tight. And for the first time in a long time, I let myself cry in front of her.

The kind of cry that shakes your shoulders, that empties you out from the inside.

Because in that moment, I realized something: I was still here. I was still breathing. And I had been given another chance.

But the question was—*what was I going to do with it?*

Back to the Streets—But Different This Time

When I left the hospital, my side still aching and stitches pulling every time I moved, I went back to the same streets that nearly killed me.

But this time, I wasn't the same person.

I started moving differently. I kept my head on a swivel, my circle small, my steps intentional. I wasn't hustling just to survive anymore —I was hustling to escape.

I was building something, stacking money, investing in small studio sessions, and planting seeds for something bigger.

But the streets are like quicksand. Every step you take feels like it's pulling you deeper.

One night, standing outside that same liquor store where I almost lost my life, I had a moment of clarity.

"This can't be my legacy. This can't be the end of my story."

I had survived a bullet, survived countless close calls, survived nights where death felt like it was standing right next to me, breathing down my neck.

And if God had let me survive all of that, then there had to be a *reason.*

The Turning Point

That reason started to show itself in small ways.

•A local studio owner gave me discounted hours because he believed in my music.

•A friend introduced me to someone who had connections with a youth program looking for artists to mentor kids.

•A stranger heard one of my early tracks and told me, "Man, your story needs to be heard."

The universe was speaking to me. The signs were there.

But signs don't mean much if you don't *move.*

I threw myself into my music. Every late night, every dollar earned, every ounce of energy I had left—it all went into creating something real.

The streets had given me stories, scars, and lessons. But music? Music gave me *a way out.*

The Reflection

Years later, I found myself driving down Gratiot again. The same liquor store was still there, the same cracked pavement, the same flickering streetlights.

But I wasn't the same.

I parked my car, stepped out, and just *stood there.*

I could still see the shadows of that night—the figures, the sound of the gunshot, the smell of gunpowder in the air.

But instead of fear, I felt *gratitude.*

Gratitude for the second chance. Gratitude for the pain that pushed me to change. Gratitude for the fire that had been lit in me that night— a fire that still burns to this day.

I whispered into the night air, "Thank you."

Because sometimes, survival isn't about strength. Sometimes, it's about **grace.**

The Lesson

This chapter of my life taught me something I'll never forget:

Life doesn't owe you anything. Every breath you take is a blessing. Every chance you get is a gift. And every moment you survive is proof that you've still got work to do.

I walked back to my car, shut the door, and stared out the windshield at the city lights.

The same streets that tried to bury me had given me a purpose.

And I wasn't done yet.

43
the weight of silence

There's a sound you never forget—the silence after a gunshot, the quiet in a courtroom after a judge gives their verdict, the stillness of a hospital room when you wake up alone. Silence isn't empty; it's *loud*. It carries every unspoken word, every missed opportunity, every regret.

But the heaviest silence? It's the silence inside your own mind. The silence that creeps in when the world stops moving, when the noise fades, and you're left alone with your thoughts.

This chapter isn't about music, or workshops, or the streets. It's about the moments in between—the moments where the silence felt louder than the chaos ever did.

The Stillness After the Storm

After surviving the shooting, after leaving the hospital with stitches in my side and fresh scars on my soul, something changed in me. Not just physically—but *mentally*.

The world felt… different. Colors weren't as bright. Laughter didn't hit the same. Even music felt hollow for a while.

Trauma has a way of reshaping your mind without asking for permission.

For weeks, I couldn't sleep without seeing flashes of that night—the faces, the gun, the feeling of blood soaking through my clothes. When I did fall asleep, the nightmares woke me up gasping for air, drenched in sweat, clutching my side like the wound had reopened.

But the worst part wasn't the nightmares—it was the silence when I was awake.

Because in that silence, the questions crept in:

- *Why am I still here?*
- *What if I had died that night?*
- *Am I really doing enough with this second chance?*

I didn't have answers. And the silence didn't offer any.

A Silent Drive to Nowhere

One night, unable to sleep, I grabbed my keys, walked out to my cream Chevy Caprice, and started driving. No destination, no plan. Just me, the car, and the road.

The city felt different at night—quieter, colder. Streetlights flickered, and shadows danced along the sidewalks. Every empty block felt like a reflection of the emptiness I was carrying inside.

I ended up parking by the riverfront. The water was calm, the moon reflecting on its surface like a cracked mirror. I sat on the hood of my car, staring out over the water, letting the cold air bite at my skin.

For a long time, I didn't move.

I thought about Sean, about the night 20 gang members came to our house, about the way my mom fired that AK-47 into the sky without hesitation.

I thought about my best friend's funeral and the weight of survivor's guilt that still sat heavy on my chest.

And I thought about my kids—Imani, Pepper, and Terrell. Wondering if they were okay. Wondering if they missed me. Wondering if they knew how much I loved them.

The silence grew louder and louder until it felt like it was screaming at me.

"Do something. Move. Fight. Build."

I took a deep breath and let it out slowly.

I didn't have all the answers that night, but I knew one thing: I couldn't let this silence consume me.

The Mask We Wear

On the outside, I looked fine. I showed up to dice games, to the workshops, to family gatherings, wearing the same mask I had perfected over the years.

The *"I'm good"* mask. The *"Nothing bothers me"* mask.

But on the inside, I was breaking.

Nobody tells you how heavy it is to carry your own trauma while trying to be strong for everyone else. Nobody tells you that healing isn't linear—that some days you'll feel fine, and others, you'll feel like you're drowning in an ocean of your own thoughts.

But the streets don't give you space to break down. They don't hand out permission slips for vulnerability. So, I buried it. I shoved it all deep inside, locked it up and threw away the key.

But pain doesn't disappear just because you ignore it. It waits. It festers. And eventually, it *explodes*.

The Breakdown

It happened late one night after a workshop. The kids had been incredible that day—sharing their verses, opening up, and creating this raw, beautiful energy in the room. But after everyone left and the lights turned off, I sat in the empty classroom, my head in my hands.

Everything hit me at once. The shooting. The funerals. The silence of courtrooms. The absence of my kids. The weight of trying to save everyone while feeling like I couldn't even save myself.

I broke down.

I cried the way I hadn't cried since I was a kid—deep, heavy sobs that felt like they were being pulled from the pit of my stomach.

And in that moment, sitting alone in that empty room, I realized something:

I had to let go of the weight I was carrying. I had to face it, name it, and start healing from it. Because if I didn't, it was going to destroy me.

The First Step Toward Healing

Healing isn't a straight line. It's not a movie montage where everything gets better in two minutes. It's messy. It's painful. And sometimes, it feels impossible.

But I started trying.

I started journaling—not just writing songs, but writing *everything*.

The ugly thoughts, the fears, the regrets. I put them down on paper so they couldn't live rent-free in my head anymore.

I started talking—not just to the kids in the workshops, but to people I trusted. I let myself be *honest.* I let myself admit that I wasn't okay.

And slowly—so slowly it was almost invisible—I started feeling *lighter.*

The silence wasn't so loud anymore. The weight wasn't so crushing.

Turning Pain into Power

One day, during a workshop, a young boy shared a verse he had written about losing his older brother. His voice cracked halfway through, and he stopped, looking down at the floor, tears pooling in his eyes.

I walked over to him, put my hand on his shoulder, and said:

"It's okay, bro. Let it out. You don't have to hold it in here."

He nodded, wiped his face, and finished his verse.

After the session, he came up to me and said, *"Thank you. I never told anyone that before."*

That's when I realized: healing isn't just something we do for ourselves—it's something we share with others.

The Lesson in the Silence

Looking back, I realize now that the silence wasn't trying to break me—it was trying to *teach* me.

It taught me to slow down.

It taught me to listen—to myself, to others, to God.

It taught me that vulnerability isn't weakness—it's *strength.*

The silence taught me that healing isn't about forgetting the past— it's about *learning to live with it.*

The Road Ahead

The silence still visits me sometimes. Late at night, when the world is quiet and the weight of everything creeps back in.

But now? Now I know how to sit with it. I know how to listen to it. And I know how to let it go.

Because every time I step into a workshop, every time I hand a kid a mic, every time I hear a young voice crack with raw emotion—I remember:

This is why I survived. This is why I'm still here.

The silence isn't something to fear anymore. It's just another part of the story.

And my story?

It's far from over.

44

the business of survival

*S*urviving the streets is one thing—building a legacy is another. Survival teaches you to live moment by moment, but legacy forces you to think ahead. When I started focusing on *World of Music*, it wasn't just about workshops and verses—it was about creating something *sustainable*. Something that could outlive me.

But no one tells you how hard it is to turn passion into a *business*. No one tells you that your biggest fight isn't with your past—it's with the system, with doubt, and sometimes... with *yourself*.

From Hustler to Entrepreneur

I've always been a hustler. Whether it was dice games behind liquor stores, flipping cars, or stacking cash on the road, I knew how to make money. But business? Business was different. Contracts, budgets, sponsorships, grant proposals—it felt like learning a foreign language.

I remember sitting at my kitchen table late one night, papers spread out in front of me—grant applications, budget sheets, event proposals. The numbers didn't make sense, the jargon was confusing, and my head was pounding.

"Man, I'm not cut out for this."

But then I stopped myself. I had survived bullets. I had survived betrayal. I had survived losing my best friend. There was no way I was letting a stack of papers take me out.

So I started studying:

- Watching YouTube videos about non-profit management.
- Reading books about building sustainable programs.
- Sitting down with people who had experience and *listening*.

Slowly, I started figuring it out. The same focus I brought to dice games, I brought to spreadsheets. The same hunger I brought to hustling, I brought to building partnerships.

And little by little, *World of Music* started to look less like a passion project and more like an organization with a purpose.

The Grant That Almost Broke Me

There was one grant—one *big* grant—that could've changed everything. It would've paid for new equipment, covered travel expenses, and secured workshops for an entire year. I spent weeks on that application. Late nights, early mornings, cross-referencing every dollar, every detail.

When I finally hit "Submit," I let out a breath I didn't even realize I was holding.

Weeks passed. No word.

Then, one day, the email came.

"We regret to inform you that your application has not been selected for funding."

I stared at the screen, the words blurring as tears stung my eyes. I had done *everything* right. I had followed every rule, double-checked every number, poured my heart into every sentence.

And it still wasn't enough.

For a moment, I felt like giving up. Like maybe they were right—maybe this wasn't sustainable. Maybe *I* wasn't enough.

But then I remembered something I had learned from the streets:

When you lose, you don't stop playing. You learn, and you come back harder.

I closed the laptop, wiped my face, and said out loud:

"Alright. Back to work."

The Hustle Reimagined

Running *World of Music* started feeling like running the most important dice game of my life. Every dollar was a bet, every decision a roll, and every connection an opportunity. But unlike the streets, this hustle wasn't about me—it was about the *kids*.

So I started thinking like a hustler again, but this time with a *bigger vision*:

•Hosting community fundraising events with performances by the kids.

•Selling merchandise—T-shirts, hoodies, hats with the *World of Music* logo.

•Offering online workshops for kids who couldn't attend in person.

I wasn't waiting for someone to hand me an opportunity. I was *creating* them.

The money started coming in—not in stacks, not in overnight miracles, but in small, steady streams. And each dollar felt like a win because I knew where it was going.

The Roadblocks Nobody Talks About

But let me tell you something people don't talk about enough: jealousy.

Not everyone wants to see you succeed. Some people smiled in my face and shook my hand, but behind closed doors? They were plotting. Talking. Undermining.

"You think you're better than us now, huh?"

"Why you acting like a schoolteacher? You ain't no role model."

"Bro, you really think this music program gonna change anything?"

At first, those words stung. But then I realized something: People will always talk when they see you doing something they're too scared to try themselves.

I stopped explaining myself. I stopped defending my vision. Because the truth was written in every kid who stepped up to a mic and spoke their truth.

Their voices were my receipts.

Balancing Fatherhood and Purpose

Through all of this, my heart still ached for my kids—Imani, Pepper, and Terrell.

There were nights I sat in my car after workshops, staring at their pictures, wondering if they'd be proud of me. Wondering if they knew their dad was out here fighting every single day to build something for them.

The court hearings, the phone calls that never came, the letters that went unanswered—it felt like a wound that would never fully heal. But instead of letting that wound consume me, I used it as fuel.

"One day," I promised myself. *"One day, they're going to see everything I built. And they'll know it was all for them."*

The First Big Payoff

Months later, I hosted a World of Music showcase—the biggest one yet.

We had sponsors. We had volunteers. We had cameras. And most importantly? We had *the kids*.

The room was packed. Parents filled the seats, teachers stood in the back, and kids paced nervously backstage, clutching their lyric sheets.

When the first kid stepped on stage and started rapping, the crowd went silent. His voice was steady, his words raw, his message clear.

"I ain't what they say I am / I'm more than these streets, I got bigger plans / The mic my weapon, the words my shield / I'm here to speak, I'm here to heal."

The crowd erupted.

I stood in the back, arms crossed, eyes glassy, heart full.

This wasn't just a showcase. It was proof. Proof that the dream was real. Proof that the work was worth it.

The Lesson in the Hustle

That night, as I locked up the venue and loaded the equipment into my car, I realized something:

- The streets had taught me *survival*.
- Music had taught me *expression*.
- But *World of Music*? It was teaching me a *legacy*.

This wasn't just a hustle. It wasn't just a program. It wasn't just a dream.

It was a movement.

And I was just getting started.

45

the mirror and the mask

The most dangerous enemy I ever faced wasn't a man with a gun, a courtroom judge, or a crooked system. It was myself —the man staring back at me in the mirror. The version of me that carried every scar, every loss, every regret like bricks in a backpack I refused to put down.

People say time heals all wounds, but they're wrong. Time doesn't heal—truth does.

And the truth is, for a long time, I was scared to face myself. Scared to pull off the mask I had worn for so many years—the mask of survival, the mask of strength, the mask of "I'm good."

But eventually, every mask starts to crack.

The Quiet Before the Fall

It started subtly. Little cracks in the armor. Days when I couldn't get out of bed. Nights when I couldn't close my eyes without hearing the echo of gunshots or seeing flashes of faces I'd lost along the way.

I was running *World of Music*, hosting workshops, inspiring kids, and from the outside, it looked like I was *winning*.

But inside, I was unraveling.

I kept telling myself, *"I'm fine. I'll deal with it later."*

But later never came. Because when you're always moving, when you're always grinding, when you're always focused on the next task, you never stop long enough to check on yourself.

Until your body makes you stop.

When the Body Keeps Score

One afternoon, I was in the middle of a workshop. The kids were writing verses, the beat was playing in the background, and everything felt… normal.

But out of nowhere, my chest tightened. My vision blurred. My hands started shaking.

I leaned against the table, trying to catch my breath, but it felt like there was an elephant sitting on my chest.

"Mr. Grier, are you okay?" one of the kids asked, his voice full of concern.

I nodded, forcing a smile. "Yeah, man. I'm good. Just need some air."

But I wasn't good. I wasn't even close to good.

I stepped outside, leaned against the brick wall of the school building, and slid down until I was sitting on the ground. My head was spinning, my heart racing, and for the first time in my life, I thought: *Is this it? Is this how it ends?*

Facing the Mirror

I didn't die that day. But something in me did—the illusion that I could carry it all without breaking.

That night, I sat in front of a mirror in my bathroom, staring at my own reflection. My face looked older, tired, and worn. My eyes were bloodshot, and the weight of everything I had been carrying was written all over my skin.

"Who are you, man?" I whispered to myself. "What are you even doing anymore?"

That question lingered in the air, heavy and sharp.

I realized then that I had spent so much time pouring into others— into the kids, into *World of Music*, into my vision—that I had left myself *empty*.

You can't pour from an empty cup. But I had been trying to for years.

The Breaking Point

The next day, I did something I had never done before: I called for help.

I reached out to an old mentor of mine—a man who had been through his own battles and come out the other side.

We met at a quiet diner on the outskirts of town. Two cups of coffee sat between us, steam rising into the space between heavy silence.

"What's going on?" he asked, his voice calm but firm.

And for the first time in years, I told someone everything.

The nightmares. The breakdowns. The exhaustion. The guilt. The fear of failure. The fear of success. The fear of not being enough for my kids, for the kids in *World of Music*, for myself.

He listened. He didn't interrupt. He didn't judge. He just… listened.

When I finished, he leaned back in his chair and said, "You've been carrying a weight that wasn't meant for one man to carry. It's okay to put some of it down."

His words hit me like a punch to the chest. Because deep down, I knew he was right.

The Healing Begins

Healing isn't pretty. It's not inspirational quotes on Instagram or self-help books with glossy covers. It's ugly. It's painful. It's messy.

I started therapy. Yeah, therapy. Something I never thought I'd do.

At first, I hated it. Sitting in a room with someone who didn't know me, didn't know my struggles, asking me to *talk about my feelings*? It felt pointless.

But over time, I started to open up. I started to unpack the trauma I had buried so deep I didn't even realize it was still there.

I talked about the night my best friend died.

I talked about being shot.

I talked about the courts keeping my kids away from me.

I talked about the guilt, the anger, the fear.

And slowly, brick by brick, I started taking off the mask.

Back to the Mission

Healing didn't mean stopping. It didn't mean quitting. It meant showing up as a better version of myself—for me, for my kids, for *World of Music*, for everyone counting on me.

I started bringing a different energy to the workshops. I wasn't just showing the kids how to express themselves—I was showing them that it's okay to hurt. It's okay to be vulnerable. It's okay to heal.

One day, a young boy in a workshop asked me, "Mr. Grier, have you ever been scared?"

I paused, took a deep breath, and said, "Yeah, man. All the time. But fear isn't the enemy. It's what you do *with* that fear that matters."

His eyes lit up like he had just heard something that changed his world. And in that moment, I realized: My scars weren't weaknesses—they were proof that healing is possible.

The Lesson in the Mirror

Healing is a journey, not a destination. There are still nights when the silence creeps back in, when the weight feels heavy, when the mirror shows me things I'd rather not see.

But now, I face it. I don't run from it.

Because I know one thing for sure: If I don't heal, I can't help others heal. And that's what this mission is all about.

I stood in front of the mirror one night, looked myself in the eyes, and said:

"You survived the streets. You survived the bullets. You survived the guilt. You survived yourself. You're still here for a reason. Now act like it."

And I did.

46
the burden of forgiveness

orgiveness is one of the hardest things you'll ever have to do—not because of the person you're forgiving, but because of *you*. The anger, the resentment, the memories—they build walls inside your chest, and every brick is laid by your own hands. But forgiveness? Forgiveness is taking those walls down brick by brick, knowing it won't be easy, and doing it anyway.

But before I could forgive anyone else, I had to start with myself.

The Mirror Never Lies

The thing about healing is that it doesn't let you hide. It strips you bare, holds you in front of a mirror, and forces you to face every version of yourself—the scared kid, the reckless teenager, the broken man.

And let me tell you, standing in front of that mirror wasn't easy.

I saw every mistake. Every wrong turn. Every moment where I could've done better but didn't.

I saw the hurt in my kids' eyes when they realized I wasn't coming home.

I saw the tears on my mother's face after the shooting.

I saw the graves of friends who didn't make it out, their names etched in stone while I was still here, breathing.

Why me? That question haunted me more than any ghost ever could.

But here's the thing about forgiveness—it doesn't come all at once. It starts with a single decision. A single whisper in the dark:

"I deserve to heal."

I had to remind myself that I was more than my mistakes. That my past didn't have to be a life sentence. That my scars didn't have to define me—they could *guide* me.

The People I Couldn't Save

There's a special kind of guilt that comes from surviving when others didn't. When you make it out of the fire, but the people you love get burned alive.

I used to replay their faces in my mind—the friends I buried, the brothers I lost to bullets and bad decisions. Each face was like a weight strapped to my chest.

One friend in particular stuck with me—my best friend, who died at 15.

I remember standing at his grave, the sky heavy with clouds, the air sharp and cold. I couldn't cry. I just stood there, staring at his name carved into the stone, feeling like it should've been mine.

"I'm sorry, bro."

Those words came out of my mouth so many times over the years. I whispered them in empty rooms, screamed them into the night, wrote them in verses that no one would ever hear.

But no amount of "I'm sorry" could bring him back.

I had to realize that his death wasn't my fault. The streets took him, the same way they tried to take me. But I was still here, and if I was still here, then I had a *responsibility* to make it mean something.

The Father I Never Knew

Forgiveness isn't just about the people who hurt you—it's about the people who *weren't there*.

I used to carry so much anger toward my father. The man who wasn't around. The man who left me and my mom to figure it out on our own.

That anger turned into a fire that fueled so many of my decisions—some good, most bad.

But one day, while sitting alone with my thoughts, I realized something: He was just a man. A flawed, broken man who didn't know how to stay.

Maybe he was scared.

Maybe he was lost.

Maybe he carried his own weight, his own demons, his own regrets.

I'll never know. But what I do know is that carrying that anger wasn't hurting him—it was *hurting me*.

So I let it go.

I didn't do it for him. I did it for *me*. Because carrying that weight was keeping me from moving forward. And I had places to go.

The Weight of Being a Father Myself

Becoming a father changes everything. It shifts your perspective, your priorities, your purpose. But being a father while carrying *guilt*, *shame*, and *regret*? That's a weight nobody prepares you for.

My kids—Imani, Pepper, and Terrell—deserved more from me. They deserved more time, more presence, more of *me*.

But the system took that away. Courtrooms with judges who didn't see me as a father—they saw me as a statistic. Paperwork that said I wasn't fit to raise my own blood.

For years, I let that anger eat away at me. Every missed birthday, every unanswered phone call, every time I whispered their names before falling asleep—it all felt like punishment.

But one day, I realized something:

I couldn't change the past, but I could build a future.

Every workshop I ran, every kid I mentored, every verse I wrote— it was all for them. It was all to build something so undeniable, so powerful, that one day they'd look at me and say, *"That's my dad. And I'm proud of him."*

The Ones Who Didn't Deserve Forgiveness

Now, let me be honest: not everyone deserves forgiveness.

There are people who crossed lines that can never be uncrossed. People who betrayed me in ways that still make my stomach turn. People who looked me in the eyes and smiled while holding a knife behind their back.

Forgiveness doesn't mean forgetting. It doesn't mean letting those people back into your life. It means *freeing yourself* from the chains of anger and resentment they left you with.

I didn't forgive them for them—I forgave them for *me*.

Because carrying that poison in my chest wasn't hurting them—it was *killing me*.

So I let it go. I didn't forget, but I let go. And in doing so, I took back my power.

The Road to Redemption

Forgiveness isn't the end of the story—it's just another chapter.

It doesn't erase the past, but it lets you move forward without dragging the weight of it behind you.

I had to forgive:

•My father, for not being there.

•Myself, for the mistakes I made.

•The streets, for taking so many people I loved.

•The system, for failing me and my kids.

But most importantly, I had to choose healing every single day.

Because forgiveness isn't a one-time thing—it's a decision you make over and over again.

A Letter to My Younger Self

If I could go back and talk to that scared, angry kid on Hickory Street, I'd tell him this:

"You're going to make mistakes. You're going to hurt people, and you're going to get hurt. But don't let the weight of it crush you. Don't let the anger eat you alive. Because one day, you're going to build something beautiful. One day, you're going to break cycles. One day, you're going to forgive yourself. And when you do, the world will start to open up in ways you can't even imagine."

The Lesson in Forgiveness

Forgiveness isn't weakness—it's *freedom*.

It doesn't mean you forget. It doesn't mean you excuse. It means you *release*.

And when you release that weight, you make space—for healing, for love, for peace.

I'm still learning. I'm still healing. But every day, I get a little lighter.

Because forgiveness isn't just something you give others—it's something you *give yourself*.

And I've finally started to accept that I deserve it.

47

when the world stops listening

There's a moment in every journey when the applause dies down, the lights dim, and the room empties out. You're left standing there, staring into the silence, wondering if the world has stopped listening.

For a long time, everything with *World of Music* felt like it was moving upward. More schools, more kids, more opportunities. But life has a way of testing you when you least expect it.

When the calls slowed down, when the grants stopped coming in, when the workshops became harder to book—I found myself staring at an empty calendar and an even emptier bank account.

But here's the thing about moments like that: they reveal who you are when nobody's watching.

The Empty Calendar

It started slow. A school canceled a workshop. Another pushed back a scheduled event. A sponsor backed out at the last minute.

At first, I brushed it off. *"It's just a slow season."*

But weeks turned into months, and the silence became louder.

One afternoon, I sat at my desk, staring at my phone. No new emails. No missed calls. Nothing.

I felt useless. Like everything I had built was slipping through my fingers, and there was nothing I could do to stop it.

"Did I fail? Did I do something wrong? Was this it?"

Those thoughts circled my mind like vultures, picking at every bit of confidence I had left.

The Conversation That Broke Me

One night, I met up with an old friend. Someone who had seen me at my lowest and celebrated me at my highest.

We were sitting in my car, the engine humming softly, the air thick with silence.

"I feel like I'm losing it, man," I said, my voice barely above a whisper.

He nodded slowly, staring out the windshield. "You ever think about why you started all this in the first place?"

"Yeah," I said. "For the kids. For my kids. For myself."

"Then keep going," he said. "You're looking at the calendar, but you're forgetting what you've already done. You've already changed lives, man. Don't let a slow season make you forget that."

His words hit me hard. Because he was right.

The calendar might've been empty, but the impact? That was *full*.

The Hustle Reimagined—Again

When the world stops listening, you have two choices:

1. You can sit in the silence and let it consume you.

2. Or you can make *noise* until they have no choice but to hear you.

I chose the second one.

I went back to the basics. I picked up the phone, made calls, sent emails, showed up uninvited to meetings, and pitched *World of Music* like it was the most important thing on earth—because to me, it was.

I recorded videos of the kids performing and sent them to potential sponsors. I created new program proposals, tighter budgets, and clearer plans for expansion.

But most importantly? I didn't stop moving.

The streets taught me one thing: *When you're losing, you double down.*

A Workshop That Changed Everything

One day, I got a call from a small community center I had worked with years ago.

"Hey, we had someone drop out last minute. Can you come in and run a workshop next week?"

I didn't hesitate. "Absolutely."

When I walked into that gym, it felt like coming home. The smell of old sneakers and faint cleaning chemicals, the sound of kids laughing in the distance—it was all familiar.

The kids shuffled in, most of them slouched in their chairs, heads down, phones in their hands.

But by the end of the session? They were *alive.*

They were writing. They were sharing. They were rapping into the mic with fire in their voices.

One kid—let's call him Tyrell—stood up and rapped a verse that stopped me cold:

"My pops been gone, my momma cryin' every night / But when I write these bars, man, I start to see the light / They told me I'm nothin', they told me I'm stuck / But look at me now, man, I'm finally standin' up."

When he finished, the room went silent for a moment. Then the applause came.

But the part I'll never forget? After the workshop, he walked up to me, looked me dead in the eyes, and said:

"Thank you for showing up, man. I needed this today."

That's when I realized: The calendar might be empty, but the mission is still alive.

The Loneliness of Leadership

When you're leading something—whether it's a movement, a business, or a family—there's a loneliness that comes with it.

You're the one who has to stay strong when everyone else is falling apart. You're the one who has to believe when everyone else is doubting.

But who do you turn to when *you* need someone to lean on?

I started leaning on my team more. Delegating. Trusting.

I started leaning on my faith more. Praying. Listening.

And I started leaning on *myself* more. Reminding myself of the nights I had survived, the losses I had overcome, and the fire that still burned in my chest.

The Spark Returns

One day, out of nowhere, I got an email from a statewide youth conference asking if I'd be interested in being a keynote speaker.

My hands shook as I read the email.

"We've been following your work with World of Music, and we'd love for you to share your story with our audience."

It was the opportunity I had been praying for.

And when I stood on that stage weeks later, looking out at hundreds of faces—educators, kids, community leaders—I knew one thing for certain:

The world hadn't stopped listening. It was just waiting for me to speak louder.

The Lesson in the Silence

That season of silence taught me something I'll never forget:

•Purpose isn't seasonal. Even when the world stops clapping, the mission remains.

•Impact doesn't expire. The lives you've changed are forever changed.

•Keep moving. Slow seasons aren't the end—they're a test.

That chapter of stillness refined me. It forced me to remember *why* I started and *who* I was doing this for.

And when the noise came back, when the opportunities started flowing again, I was ready.

Because I had survived the silence.

48

the legacy blueprint

*B*uilding something that outlasts you isn't about money, fame, or applause—it's about **impact**. It's about planting seeds in people who will never forget your name, not because you told them to, but because you *showed up* when they needed you the most.

At this point in my life, *World of Music* wasn't just a program—it was a *movement*. A living, breathing testament to what happens when you mix raw pain with relentless purpose. But movements don't sustain themselves—they require *leaders*. They require *vision*. And they require you to be bold enough to see beyond yourself.

The Next Generation

One of the hardest truths I had to face was this: I can't do this forever.

Not because I wanted to stop, but because every great leader knows when it's time to pass the torch.

During one workshop, I noticed one of my oldest participants—a girl named Kayla—pulling a group of younger kids aside and helping them with their verses. She was patient and kind and had a fire in her eyes that reminded me of myself when I first started.

After the session, I pulled her aside.

"You ever thought about leading one of these workshops yourself?" I asked.

Her eyes went wide. "Me? Lead a workshop? Mr. Grier, I'm not ready for that."

"Yes, you are," I said firmly. "You've been ready. You just need someone to tell you."

The following week, I handed her the mic—not to rap, but to lead.

Watching her guide those kids, hearing her encourage them, seeing her confidence grow with every word—it hit me.

This was the beginning of something bigger than me.

Scaling the Dream

I started thinking bigger. Not just about workshops, but about systems—ways to ensure *World of Music* could exist without me being in every single room.

I laid out a plan:

•Train youth leaders like Kayla to run workshops.

•Build an online platform where kids from anywhere could access music programs.

•Host annual showcases that brought kids, schools, and supporters together.

•Create a scholarship fund for kids pursuing music education.

The dream wasn't just about reaching kids in my city anymore—it was about reaching kids *everywhere*.

I wanted *World of Music* to become a blueprint for other leaders, other dreamers, other people who believed in the power of storytelling through music.

A Visit That Changed Everything

One day, while visiting one of our newer workshops, a young boy —no older than 10—walked up to me after everyone had left.

He was small, wearing sneakers two sizes too big, with a backpack that hung low on his shoulders.

"Mr. Grier," he said, his voice barely above a whisper. "You saved me, you know?"

I froze.

"What do you mean, little man?"

"My big brother… he's locked up. My dad's gone. But when I'm here, when I'm writing, I don't feel so alone. You saved me."

I crouched down to his level, looked him dead in the eyes, and said:

"You saved *yourself*, kid. I just gave you the mic."

As he walked away, I realized something: This is what legacy feels like. It's not about how many people know your name—it's about how many lives you've touched.

And I wasn't done yet.

The Full Circle Moment

Life has a way of bringing you back to where you started—not as a punishment, but as a reminder of how far you've come.

One evening, I found myself driving down Hickory Street. The same street where my brother Sean had stood his ground against the 7 Mile Bloods. The same street where my mom fired warning shots into the sky to protect her family.

I parked my car and just… sat there.

The street was quieter now, but the ghosts of those nights still lingered in the corners.

I closed my eyes and whispered, *"Look at us now."*

The Dream Lives On

The final *World of Music* showcase of the year was held in a packed auditorium.

Kids from different neighborhoods, different schools, and different walks of life stood on that stage and told their stories.

Some rapped about loss.

Some sang about hope.

Some shared verses about dreams bigger than their circumstances.

But every voice had one thing in common: courage.

I stood at the back of the room, tears welling up in my eyes as I watched them.

This wasn't just a program anymore. This was a movement. A legacy. A revolution built on stories, beats, and microphones.

And the craziest part? It was *still growing*.

A Message to My Kids

Before this book ends, there's something I need to say to my kids— Imani, Pepper, and Terrell:

"I know I wasn't there in all the ways I should've been. I know the system tried to build walls between us, but I need you to know this: Every breath I've taken, every move I've made, every verse I've written—it's all been for you. To build something you can be proud of. To show you that no matter where you come from, no matter how hard life hits, you can rise. I love you with every fiber of my being. And one day, I hope you'll stand on this foundation I've built and reach even higher than I ever could."

The Final Verse

If there's one thing I want you, the reader, to take away from this story, it's this:

Your pain has a purpose. Your scars have stories. And your voice—no matter how small it feels—can shake mountains.

I'm not done. This isn't the end. It's just the final chapter of this *book*.

Because the work, the dream, the mission…

It's still moving. It's still growing. And it's still changing lives.

And if you've been with me on this journey, if you've felt even an ounce of what I've poured into these pages, then know this:

You're part of the story now, too.

So pick up the mic. Speak your truth. Write your verse.

Because the world needs your voice.

The Mic Drops, but the Beat Goes On

I closed my notebook, leaned back in my chair, and exhaled.

This isn't the end of my story.

It's just the beginning of *yours*.

Thank you for listening. Thank you for reading. And thank you for believing.

See you in the next chapter of life.

Mic drop.

49

the final chapter – but not the end

*E*very story needs an ending, but not every ending means it's over. This chapter isn't about closing doors—it's about leaving them wide open. It's about letting the light spill into the places that were once shadowed by fear, doubt, and pain.

This isn't the end of my story—it's the end of this *book*. The pen is just pausing, not stopping. And as I write these final words, I want to leave you with something real. Something raw. Something you can carry with you long after you close these pages.

The Road Behind Me

When I look back, it feels like a movie reel playing in my head—scenes flashing one after another:

•The cracked pavement on Hickory Street, where my mom fired shots into the sky to protect her family.

•The smell of dice games, sweat, and adrenaline in back alleys and abandoned parking lots.

•The sharp sting of bullets, the cold floor of an emergency room, and the flickering hospital lights overhead.

•The faces of my kids, the weight of their absence, and the fire in my chest to build something *for them*.

•The first mic I handed to a kid in a workshop, and the way their voice cracked as they spoke their truth into the world.

All of it—the pain, the loss, the victories, the scars—built me into the man I am today.

Every moment mattered. Every moment taught me something.

But the road behind me isn't what defines me. It's the road *ahead* that keeps me moving.

The Road Ahead

There's still so much work to do.

•World of Music isn't finished—it's evolving. I want to see it in every school, every community center, every corner of the world where a kid feels invisible.

•I want to build a foundation for my kids—something they can stand on, grow from, and pass down to their own children one day.

•I want to create **opportunities for other leaders**—young people with vision, drive, and stories of their own to tell.

But most importantly, I want to keep showing up.

Because showing up is half the battle. And in a world where so many people don't, showing up is a revolution all on its own.

To the Ones Who Didn't Make It

Before I close this book, I need to take a moment for the ones who didn't make it.

To my best friend, whose life was cut short before he could see what was waiting for him.

To every brother I've buried, every funeral I've attended, every tear I've shed.

To every kid who didn't get the chance to speak their truth into a mic or tell their story to someone who would listen.

Your voices live on in me.

Every verse I write. Every workshop I run. Every stage I stand on.

You are with me. Always.

A Final Letter to My Kids

To Imani, Pepper, and Terrell:

If you're reading this one day, know this—you were always the reason.

Every sacrifice, every sleepless night, every risk I took—it was all for you.

The world tried to keep us apart. The system tried to convince me I wasn't enough. But I fought every day to prove them wrong.

I hope you're proud of me. I hope you see yourself in the work I've done, in the lives I've touched, and in the legacy I've built.

But more than anything, I hope you know this:

I love you. Always have. Always will.

No matter how far, no matter how long—you were, and always will be, my greatest purpose.

To the Reader

If you've made it to this point, thank you.

Thank you for listening.

Thank you for believing.

Thank you for walking this road with me.

This isn't just *my* story—it's *ours*.

Because every struggle, every loss, every victory—it's universal. It's raw. It's real.

And if there's one thing I want you to take from these pages, it's this:

Your story matters. Your voice matters. You matter.

Whatever fire is burning inside you, don't let it go out.

Speak your truth. Build your legacy. Leave something behind that the world can feel long after you're gone.

The Final Scene

I'm standing on a stage, staring out at a packed auditorium. The kids are in the front row—eyes wide, notebooks open, ready to soak in every word.

Behind them, parents, teachers, and community members fill every seat. The lights are bright, the mic is warm in my hand, and the air buzzes with anticipation.

I lean forward, look out into the crowd, and say:

"Every single one of you has a story. Every single one of you has a voice. And the world needs to hear it. Don't let fear stop you. Don't let doubt silence you. Don't let anyone tell you your story doesn't matter. Because it does. It always has. It always will."

The crowd erupts into applause.

But I'm not focused on the noise—I'm focused on the faces.

Because in every face, I see possibility. I see a purpose. I see *the future.*

The Mic Drops, But the Story Doesn't End

This is where this book ends, but it's not where the story stops.

The beat keeps playing.

The mic stays open.

The mission continues.

And as long as there's breath in my lungs and fire in my chest, I'm going to keep showing up.

For the kids.

For my kids.

For the people who never got the chance.

For the ones who are still fighting.

And for myself.

Because this isn't just about music.

It's about legacy.

It's about love.

It's about freedom.

And it's about living a life so loud and so impactful that the world can't help but remember your name.

Thank you for listening. Thank you for believing.

See you in the next chapter of life.

Mic drop.

A Letter to My Children

To My Children,

There are so many things I want to say, so many moments I wish I could have frozen in time—your first steps, your first words, the way your eyes lit up when you saw me walk into a room. Every one of those memories is etched into my soul, a permanent reminder of why I've fought so hard to become the man I am today.

You were my reason before I even understood what it meant to have one. When the world felt heavy and the streets tried to pull me under, your faces reminded me of what I was fighting for. You were my light in the darkest moments, my anchor when the storms threatened to pull me away.

Life didn't always go the way I planned. There were times I fell short, times I stumbled, times I felt like I had let you down. But through every struggle, every setback, I carried you with me—in my mind, in my heart, in every decision I made.

I want you to know this: you are my legacy. Not the money I made, not the battles I fought, not even the businesses I built. *You.* You are my greatest achievement, my proudest moment, and my deepest joy.

The world isn't always kind, and life won't always be fair. But if there's one thing I hope you carry from my story, it's this: Never give up on yourself. Never let anyone tell you who you are or what you're worth. And never, ever stop fighting for your dreams.

You come from strength. You come from resilience. You come from love. And no matter how far apart we may be, know that I am with you in every heartbeat, every breath, every step you take.

When you feel lost, when the weight of the world feels too heavy to carry, come back to these words. Let them remind you of who you are and where you come from.

I love you endlessly, and I will always be proud of you.

With all my heart,

—Dad

epilogue
The Next Chapter

*L*ife isn't a straight path. It's a maze filled with sharp turns, dead ends, and open doors you didn't even know existed. Every scar, every tear, every victory, and every loss—they all built the person I am today.

This book isn't just the story of where I've been; it's a reflection of where I'm going. And it's a reminder to you—the one holding these pages—that your story isn't over either.

I've learned that survival isn't just about staying alive; it's about finding a reason to keep living. It's about building something that outlasts you. It's about turning every wound into wisdom and every mistake into momentum.

There were times I thought I wouldn't make it—times when the streets almost swallowed me whole, when the weight of loss felt unbearable, and when the system seemed designed to break me. But here I stand. And if you're reading this, then here *you* are, too.

We all carry something—some pain, some regret, some dream we haven't chased yet. But I'm here to tell you, it's never too late. Never too late to heal, never too late to start over, and never too late to build a life that feels like yours.

This isn't the end of my story; it's just another chapter. I still have dreams to chase, lives to impact, and lessons to learn. And so do you.

As you close this book, I hope you feel something stir inside you—a fire, a purpose, a determination to keep moving forward.

Your story is still being written. The pen is in your hand.

So go ahead—turn the page.

The world is waiting for what comes next.

The End (For Now)